The Living Body

Body

The Church Christ is Building

Dr. Richard Halverson

CHAPLAIN, UNITED STATES SENATE

VISION HOUSE PUBLISHING, INC.

Gresham, Oregon

Printed in the United States of America.

00 99 98 97 96 95 94
7 6 5 4 3 2 1

Dedication

*To my beloved wife, Doris,
and our children, Chris, Steve, and Debbie,
who, with their families, have been and continue to be
immeasurable blessings in my life.*

Contents

Contents

Acknowledgment

It would have been impossible for me to finish this manuscript except for the faithful support and work of my indespensable executive assistant, Martie Kinsell.

Chapter One

The Church in God's Sight

They devoted themselves to the apostles' teaching and to the fellowship, to the breaking of bread and to prayer.

Acts 2:42

Recently while traveling in southern Maryland, I passed an old, dilapidated church building. Once it had been a thriving rural church. Now its paint was peeled away, the windows were broken, the doors were unhinged, the steps were collapsing. The church was in general disrepair, and it had been that way for considerable time. As we passed that building I could not help feeling that if we could see as God sees, we would see what we call *the church* in a similar condition.

Perhaps the buildings are new and well constructed and attractive and powerful looking. But spiritually, the church is like the old, worn-down building in southern Maryland. And I'm not referring just to the dying churches with small attendance. I'm speaking also of the so-called super-churches with their campuses, their enormous buildings, their programs for every age, their successful senior pastors, and their swarming attendance every Sunday morning. From a secular or worldly standpoint, such a church looks successful. But I wonder if, from God's standpoint, it looks anything like he wants his church to look.

What Is the Church?

Church. How do you define it?

From my earliest years as a Christian, I was never satisfied with the definitions I was offered. Not that I felt they were wrong: some of them came from great leaders in church history, and my own experience was too limited to allow me to criticize them. But the definitions did not seem adequate.

At some point in my pilgrimage, I heard the church defined in terms of Matthew 18:20, where Christ said, "Where two or three come together in my name, there am I with them." That seemed very simple, but the more I pondered it, the more I felt it was, if not a definition, certainly a description of the church. It satisfied me more than any of the other definitions I heard through two years of college and three years of seminary.

And yet I continued to search for a definition that would help me in my ministry. Perhaps my struggle is not surprising: any definition of church is going to be inadequate, for in the act of defining, it limits the church's breadth and height and depth. Though the church is human, it is also divine, and it should be obvious that we cannot restrict or limit what the church is by some human definition. It was not until the early 1970s, fifteen years into my final pastorate in the Fourth Presbyterian Church, that satisfaction came.

Now, after forty years in the ordained ministry, twenty-one years of which have been in non-parish work rather than a conventional pastorate, I am moved to write down some thoughts about the church Christ is building. Nothing in this book will be revolutionary or surprising. I simply hope that the way in which I have been led to understand the church will be helpful to those who read.

The Church Christ Is Building

Some years out of seminary I began to study the Book of Acts, not simply as a scholar but as a pastor seriously seeking to understand the apostolic church. I recall how impressed I was with the description of the people of God fresh from the Pentecost experience. Luke records that the apostolic church "devoted themselves to the apostles' teaching and to the fellowship, to the breaking of bread and to prayer" (2:42).

That verse became prescriptive for me as a pastor. As I pastored a growing church in Bethesda, Maryland, a suburb of Washington, D.C., I let it set the course of our church life. It became my model for church programs, the irreducible minimum of church activity. The longer I served the church, the more I felt it described the maximum program of the church of Jesus Christ.

Luke beautifully describes the results of following that model, the community life of the apostolic church:

"Everyone was filled with awe, and many wonders and miraculous signs were done by the apostles. All the believers were together and had everything in common. Selling their possessions and goods, they gave to anyone as he had need. Every day they continued to meet together in the temple courts. They broke bread in their homes and ate together with glad and sincere hearts, praising God and enjoying the favor of all the people. And the Lord added to their number daily those who were being saved" (2:43-47).

That is a picture of the church Christ is building. But is it a picture of the Christian church today?

Bursting Wineskins

These are days of radical transition and change—probably far more radical than any of us realize. Most of the old-line denominations are losing members by the thousands and tens of thousands every year. In the last fifty years, we have seen the birth and rapid growth of so-called parachurch organizations, whose evangelism and discipleship programs have exceeded those of most of the denominations. We have seen what I believe to be a mighty visitation of God upon the church through the charismatic movement, which has transcended all the conventional labels and divisions among the people of God.

It seems to me that for some years we have been seeing the truth of one of Jesus' cryptic statements: "Neither do men pour new wine into old wineskins. If they do, the skins will burst, the wine will run out and the wineskins will be ruined" (Matthew 9:17). We have been seeing that the old institutions, the old wineskins, are unable to contain the new wine of the Spirit, and it spills out beyond the old wine-skins into the many parachurch organizations. At the same time, the old wineskins have been suffering controversy, discord, division, and an ecclesiastical bureaucracy that has more and more lost touch with the people.

The Church as Big Business

Religion has become big business in the United States. Dr. James Houston, who founded Regent College in order to equip the laity, describes our time in church history as "the period of the entrepreneur." Someone has observed that the Christian faith began in Palestine as an experience, moved to Greece and became a philosophy, moved to Rome and became an institution, moved to Europe and became a culture, and then moved to America and became an enterprise. A casual analysis of today's best-known evangelical leaders confirms that they are entrepreneurs and that one product of their efforts is institutions. They are the builders of great organizations that are run as big business.

Now there is nothing intrinsically wrong with entrepreneurs or big business or institutions, and one cannot easily justify criticism of them in our culture. But it is just possible that this is at the heart of the matter: the churches have become so much a part of our culture in terms of bigness and success that they are now acceptable. They conform. All the accoutrements of big business characterize them: powerful chief executive officers and chief administrative officers, a management hierarchy, concern for cost effectiveness, the bottom-line syndrome. Goals are considered essential, and goals must be measurable.

Measurableness requires criteria, and criteria demand visibility and quantification. Hence quantitative results become the measure of the movement and the basis upon which support is solicited.

Is it not conceivable that today's successful churches reflect our culture to such an extent that they are one with it and indistinguishable from it?

Some Things Cannot Be Measured

In all this talk of quantity, where is the quality of life Christ outlined in the beatitudes? How do you measure meekness, purity of heart, poverty of spirit, hunger and thirst for righteousness? What is the cost effectiveness of a godly life? What are the measurable goals in seeking the kingdom of God? How do you quantify love and sacrifice and servanthood and treating others better than yourself?

The fact is that a life of virtue and character often does not receive accolades. It may even alienate. In our culture, society often withdraws from one who lives a truly good life. Goodness and success do not go hand in hand. Indeed, they never have done so. Jesus himself was rejected by his contemporaries.

We ought to give pause at this point to think of Paul's words: "We fix our eyes not on what is seen, but on what is unseen. For what is seen is temporary, but what is unseen is eternal" (2 Corinthians 4:18). The question is not, Are these ways of measuring wrong? The question is, Do they accurately represent the one who laid down his life on a cross, rejected by his contemporaries? Do these visible, measurable results truly represent Christ's mission in the world and the church Christ is building, to whom he gave the keys of the kingdom, and which he said the gates of hell could never destroy?

Does the church in America today look anything like the apostolic church, whose people "devoted themselves to the apostles' teaching and to the fellowship, to the breaking of bread and to prayer"? What should the church look like? What is the church, in God's sight?

Chapter Two

I Will Build My Church

When Jesus came to the region of Caesarea Philippi, he asked his disciples, "Who do people say the Son of Man is?" . . . Simon Peter answered, "You are the Christ, the Son of the living God." Jesus replied, "Blessed are you, Simon son of Jonah, for this was not revealed to you by man, but by my Father in heaven. And I tell you that you are Peter, and on this rock I will build my church, and the gates of Hades will not overcome it."

Matthew 16:13, 16-18

Some fifteen years into my pastorate at Fourth Presbyterian Church in Bethesda, Maryland, a young man asked me to preach the sermon at his ordination service in a little church in Delaware. It was a privilege and an honor, and I looked forward with delight to the opportunity—even though, through the years, the least attractive part of an ordination service for me has been the sermon. An ordination service already includes a charge to the person being ordained and a charge to the congregation, and I often felt that a sermon, if not superfluous, was at least redundant. But I had agreed to preach and, in prayer, decided to prepare a message based on the familiar passage in Matthew 16 where Peter makes his great confession of faith:

"When Jesus came to the region of Caesarea Philippi, he asked his disciples, 'Who do people say the Son of Man is?' . . . Simon Peter answered, 'You are the Christ, the Son of the living God.' Jesus replied, 'Blessed are you, Simon son of Jonah, for this was not revealed to you by man, but by my Father in heaven. And I tell you that you are Peter, and on this rock I will build my church, and the gates of Hades will not overcome it'" (Matthew 16: 13, 16-18).

What Did Jesus Mean by 'Church'?

Early in the preparation of the message, I followed my usual plan of reading and rereading the passage as often as possible. As I read and pondered, a new thought came to me. What did Jesus mean by the word *church*? What was in his mind when he said it?

If I had been present and had asked Jesus what he meant when he used the word, what would he have said? How would he have explained or described or defined the word *church* in the context in which he used it?

The more I thought about it, the more I found myself saying: Whatever Jesus Christ meant when he said *church*, that is the church for me.

As simple as this sounds, this to me is still the most precise and profound answer that can be given to the question, What is the church? The church is whatever Christ meant when he used the word.

That is an excellent starting point for a complete definition of *church*, but it cannot be the end of the matter. The idea provoked me to examine the context of the passage in Matthew. It led me to study the letters of the apostle Paul, especially his letter to the Ephesians, with greater intensity than ever. I wanted to understand what was in Christ's mind when he said *church*.

The Church Is Built on Jesus Christ

In the verses surrounding the story of Peter's confession of faith, I found a number of significant clues to what Jesus meant by *church*.

The first clue is found in Jesus' words about the church's foundation or, to use the word in the passage, the "rock" upon which Jesus builds his church. This rock is Jesus himself. As Peter declared, "You are the Christ, the Son of the living God."

Peter must have had some knowledge of what he was saying when he called Jesus "the Christ" (Greek for "the anointed one"). He knew that the Jewish nation was waiting for, hoping for, the coming Messiah who would save them from their oppressors and inaugurate a new age of prosperity. Amazingly, he recognized this Galilean carpenter as the Messiah foretold in the Scriptures.

When Jesus commended Peter, he pointed out that Peter did not come to his understanding by some logical process. God revealed to him the truth that Jesus is the Christ, the Messiah, and Peter witnessed to that truth. He dared to say it aloud, as improbable as it seemed, and his witness became the rock on which Christ's church is built. The church is built upon the testimony that Jesus is the Christ, the Messiah, the Son of the living God.

Whatever Jesus meant when he used the word

church, the church must make Peter's confession its own. A group that does not make that confession, does not proclaim that Jesus is the Christ, the Son of the living God, is not the church as Christ meant it to be. *Whatever the church is, it is based upon the foundation of Jesus, the Messiah, the Son of God.*

The Church Has Jewish Roots

The second clue about the nature of Christ's church is related to the first: The church Christ is building is connected to the Jewish people. For two thousand years the world had been waiting for God's Messiah to come through Israel, ever since God promised Abraham that "all peoples on earth will be blessed through you" (Genesis 12:3). As a young Christian, I often heard this simple rhyme about the two Testaments of the Christian Bible: "The New is in the Old concealed; the Old is in the New revealed." When Jesus entered human history, this was not the beginning of a new plan on God's part. It was a continuation of the one redemptive plan that had existed in the mind of God from before the foundation of the world.

In one sense, the word "Christian" is unfortunate. It has allowed both Jews and followers of Christ to behave as though the church Christ is building is not only non-Jewish, but actually anti-Jewish. This is based on a totally false understanding. The church of the apostles was a Jewish community. Jesus was not a "Christian": he was a Jew. The church of Jesus Christ embraces all that the Old Testament teaches. New Testament believers are nurtured and edified by Old Testament truth. The church of Jesus Christ ought never to lose its Jewishness. *Whatever the church is, it is based upon God's eternal redemptive plan that was first revealed to the Jews.*

The Church Is Not an Earthly Kingdom

The story in Matthew gives a third clue about what Christ meant his church to be. This clue was so unexpected that even Peter did not understand it.

"From that time on Jesus began to explain to his disciples that he must go to Jerusalem and suffer many things at the hands of the elders, chief priests and teachers of the law, and that he must be killed and on the third day be raised to life. Peter took him aside and began to rebuke him. 'Never, Lord!' he said. 'This shall never happen to you!' Jesus turned and said to Peter, 'Get behind me, Satan! You are a stumbling block to me; you do not have in mind the things of God, but the things of men.' Then Jesus said to his disciples, 'If anyone would come after me, he must deny himself and take up his cross and follow me'" (Matthew 16:21-24).

Although Peter knew about the Messiah promised in the Hebrew Scriptures, his knowledge of the Messiah apparently did not include his humiliation, suffering, and crucifixion. Peter knew the scriptural prophecies of a conquering Messiah, but somehow the tradition ignored all the descriptions of a suffering Messiah.

No Room for the Cross

This fact becomes plain in Luke's story of the Emmaus road, found in Luke 24. On the Sunday following Jesus' death, two disciples were walking the seven miles from Jerusalem to Emmaus. The resurrected Jesus joined them. He saw the sadness in their faces as they walked and talked. He asked them what they were talking about, and they responded, "Are you the only one living in Jerusalem who doesn't know the things that have happened there in these days?"

"What things?" Jesus asked.

The disciples began to tell Jesus about their friend, Jesus of Nazareth, who had done great wonders and had been followed by many people. In the midst of their description, they said, "We had hoped that he was the one who was going to redeem Israel." In other words, we had hoped he was the Messiah prophesied in our Scriptures.

Implicit in those words was the disappointment, the frustration, the agony felt by all of Jesus' followers when he was crucified. The Messiah they were hoping for had nothing to do with crucifixion. He had nothing to do with a suffering servant. Whatever they had expected in the Messiah on the basis of their tradition, it was totally blasted when Jesus was executed. Their tradition, their expectations, their hopes had no room for the cross.

Still Waiting for the Golden Age

We see this happening again in Luke's record of the early church in Acts. Jesus had just urged his disciples not to leave Jerusalem but to wait for the promise of the Father, which he described as a baptism by the Holy Spirit. Immediately the disciples asked the question that was obviously uppermost in their minds: "Lord, are you at this time going to restore the kingdom to Israel?" (Acts 1:6).

The resurrection had erased their disillusionment

in the crucifixion. Hope had returned. But their understanding of the Messiah had not yet changed. He was to be a conquering king, a military-political Messiah. His redemptive purpose was to liberate the Jews from the Romans' cursed rule. His kingdom was earthly. No doubt they expected him to restore the golden age of Israel as it had been under King David.

But, as they were soon to learn, Jesus' expectations were not the same as theirs. Suffering and death, not worldly honor, lay ahead for many of them. The way of their Lord was the way of the cross. *Whatever the church is, it does not involve Christ's reign over an earthly kingdom.*

Salvation through Politics

This is an important fact to keep in mind at a time when many in the evangelical community are behaving as though the kingdom of God can be ushered in by political victories (or defeated by political oppression). Many seem to think that if we can just get the right person in the White House, in Congress, and on the Supreme Court, we will have the kingdom of God—or at least peace and prosperity—on earth, in the good old U.S.A.

Several years ago the noted British journalist Malcolm Muggeridge was a guest at a breakfast in Fellowship House in Washington, D.C. Following the meal, Muggeridge told of his rediscovery of Jesus, his return to Christ through the influence of Mother Teresa. When he had finished his testimony, he made a number of comments about world affairs, all of which were very pessimistic. One of the Christians present said to the speaker, "Dr. Muggeridge, you have been very pessimistic. Don't you have any reason for optimism?"

Malcolm Muggeridge replied, "My friend, I could not be more optimistic than I am, because my hope is in Jesus Christ alone." He allowed that remark to settle for a few seconds, and then he added, "Just think if the apostolic church had pinned its hope on the Roman Empire!"

Is it possible that there are those in the evangelical community who, without realizing it, are pinning their hope on a secure and prosperous United States of America, not on the return of Christ?

Tradition and Truth

Tradition can be dangerous. It can not only modify the truth; it can replace it altogether. Jesus took this danger very seriously in this conversation with the religious leaders:

"The Pharisees and teachers of the law asked Jesus, 'Why don't your disciples live according to the tradition of the elders instead of eating their food with "unclean" hands?' He replied, 'Isaiah was right when he prophesied about you hypocrites; as it is written: "These people honor me with their lips, but their hearts are far from me. They worship me in vain; their teachings are but rules taught by men." You have let go of the commands of God and are holding on to the traditions of men.' And he said to them: 'You have a fine way of setting aside the commands of God in order to observe your own traditions!' "(Mark 7:5-9).

With all our activity defending the inerrancy of the Scriptures, protesting against those who depart from the truth as taught in the Scriptures, upholding the Scriptures as the Word of God, how much have we evangelicals actually departed from God's Word because of our traditions? To what extent have we allowed our traditions to replace the Word of God in our teaching, in our activity, in our thinking? Or, to use Jesus' words, how much have we set aside the commands of God in order to observe our own traditions? Is it not possible that God's New Testament people have departed from the truth by their tradition as much as God's Old Testament people departed from the truth by theirs?

The Church Has at Its Center the Cross

The tradition believed by Jesus' followers may have ignored the biblical passages about the Messiah's suffering and death, and yet blood sacrifice is a central biblical truth, beginning with the first Passover when the blood of a lamb saved Israel's firstborn.

For hundreds of years Israel offered sacrifices to atone for their sins. How could they have missed the truth of "Calvary—the pivot upon which the whole of time and eternity turn"?[1] Tragically, it is not uncommon for religious tradition—ours as well as theirs—to eliminate the cross.

Whatever was in Jesus' mind when he used the word *church*, it certainly included his entrance into history as the Son of God to save the world by his death on the cross. If the crucifixion of Jesus Christ is rejected or removed from the church's teaching, or if it ceases to be central to the way the church sees itself, then that is not the church as Christ meant it to be. *Whatever the church is, it has at its center the cross.*

The Church Is Built by Jesus Christ

The church, then, as Jesus saw it, would be based on Jesus himself, the Messiah, the Son of God. It would fulfill God's eternal redemptive plan as proclaimed to the Old Testament patriarchs. It would not be an earthly kingdom, but would gain its power from the shame of the cross. And this church would be built by Jesus Christ himself.

"I will build my church," he told Peter and the other disciples, "and the gates of Hades will not overcome it."

Early in 1991, the morning mail in my office contained a large, slick brochure, four pages advertising a seminar for pastors to be held at a major hub city. It was an attractive piece, the kind advertising professionals use to promote workshops, seminars, or conferences. Inside were photographs of a large number of "successful" pastors and church leaders who were going to give the messages and lead the workshops. The front page screamed, in large red letters, "How to Market Your Church."

To many in the contemporary church, this kind of thinking is quite acceptable and reasonable. The church appears to be adopting the principles and practices of big business and finding these practices very effective.

Now there is nothing wrong with good business. Bad business is certainly not desirable for the church. Wise pastors and church officers will do everything they can, with care, to apply those principles and practices which maximize the effectiveness of their churches, however small or large they may be. Bigness is not evil, and smallness is not a virtue. But the question is, When do these principles and practices cease being tools for the church, when do they dominate its life to the extent that they become its master?

The church is composed of human beings redeemed by the sacrifice of Jesus Christ on the cross. It is not something we humans can build ourselves. As a matter of fact, much that we humans do to the church of Jesus Christ in our attempts to build it or improve upon it actually works the other way. Our efforts turn out to be destructive. The church becomes more and more what people are building, and less and less what Christ is building, until when we look at the church we see a totally human institution. And yet *whatever the church is, it is being built by Jesus Christ.*

Jesus Is Still Building

One unfortunate side effect of the whole big business, entrepreneurial syndrome is the way it has affected the church's mission in other countries. A great deal of what we do in the name of mission has the label "Made in the U.S.A.," and when we export it to other nations, it is simply irrelevant.

Certainly what happened in China ought to be seriously considered by the church in the West. When communism began to rule there in 1949, all missionaries were evacuated. Many pastors were imprisoned, and church buildings were closed. It was estimated, at that time, that there were one million Christian believers in China. Thirty years later when China's doors were again opened to the West, it was estimated that there were from thirty million to fifty million believers. Thirty years under Communist control and oppression, with no missionaries, pastors, or church buildings—all the accoutrements we find so essential to church growth—and the church in China grew from thirty to fifty fold.

Jesus said he would build his church. Has he been doing what he said he would do? Is he doing it now, and will he continue to do it until the consummation of God's redemptive purpose in history? Is it conceivable that Jesus might fail to do what he said he would do? Might he decide to quit building his church?

It may have seemed to the missionaries who were expelled from China in 1949 that the church of Jesus Christ there would come to an end, but the very opposite happened. Jesus kept his word. He continued building his church. In fact, somehow he was able to build it in a way that missionaries from the West had not been able to do in nearly one hundred years of effort.

The World: Love It or Leave It?

We cannot escape the tension of being in the world but not of the world (see John 17:15, 16). As human beings who are also members of Christ's church, we will often discover that our human efforts are not what Christ has in mind at all. How will we live as citizens of the kingdom of heaven, even as we live in the kingdom of this world?

At some times and in some places, parts of the church have attempted to avoid this tension by withdrawing from the world altogether, by refusing to be involved in the world in any way. There are Christians who refuse to use the products of modern technology such as electricity, telephones, and automobiles. These Christians dress differently, educate their children in their own way, and become a community withdrawn from the external world as much as is physically possible.

It is not for those of us who see differently to be critical of such conviction and the commitment to live by it. As a matter of fact, many of us, when we come in contact with such communities, feel a great nostalgia. We wonder if perhaps the frantic activity that characterizes our contemporary world is not an enemy of faith.

A more common way the church tries to avoid the tension between the kingdom of God and the world in which we live is to be as much like the world as possible, to adjust its standards and beliefs and behavior to conform to the culture around it. Often the church becomes so secularized that there is little distinction between the church and any worldly social organization.

In April 1949, the editors of *Life* magazine ran an editorial in the center spread. One paragraph was as follows: "The worst enemy western civilization faces is not communism. The worse enemy western civilization faces is within that civilization. Our $64 euphemism for it is secularism, but a much blunter word is godlessness. For all of our churches and church-goers, we have become a secular, godless civilization."

Life was prophetic: we have become so godless that no secular magazine, and few religious publications, would think of issuing such a warning today.

A Fruitful Tension

If the tension is unavoidable, it can at least be fruitful. In his high priestly prayer (John 17), our Lord asked the Father not to take us out of the world: "As you sent me into the world, I have sent them into the world," he said (verse 18). Thus we are living like pilgrims in a foreign land. Citizens of heaven, we reside in an alien world.

As pilgrims and aliens, we are following our Lord, Jesus Christ. Paul tells us that "when the time had fully come, God sent his Son . . ." (Galatians 4:4). John puts it this way: "The Word became flesh and made his dwelling among us" (1:14).

Here it is important to remind ourselves that *secular* is not a bad word. The dichotomy we often make between the secular and the sacred is not biblical. Everything that is was created by God, and he said that it was all very good. The secular world is the product of God's creation. He made it so that we could use it. God's creation belongs to his children, and we are to use it for his glory. He has given us dominion over all he has created.

The psalmist proclaimed the goodness of God's created world:

"O LORD, our Lord, how majestic is your name in all the earth! You have set your glory above the heavens. From the lips of children and infants you have ordained praise because of your enemies, to silence the foe and the avenger. When I consider your heavens, the work of your fingers, the moon and the stars, which you have set in place, what is man that you are mindful of him, the son of man that you care for him? You made him a little lower than the heavenly beings and crowned him with glory and honor. You made him ruler over the works of your hands; you put everything under his feet" (Psalm 8:1-6).

This, then, is the tension: how to be in the world, and not of it; how to be good stewards of modern developments and technology and science, and not be exploited by them; how to possess them, and not be possessed by them; how to make them the servants of Jesus and use them to the glory of God.

The Church Belongs to Jesus

Several weeks ago I received a letter from the head of a pastoral search committee of a local church, asking me to recommend candidates. From its description, the church sounded very attractive. It was in a good location, and its programs looked appealing.

Being unfamiliar with the church, however, I began to ask questions. I learned that there were a few people in this church who for years had been in total control of it. One pastor after another had been unable to fulfill the mission to which they believed God had called them. Despite their best efforts, good preaching and teaching, and competent administrative care, they were left in complete frustration. Nothing could happen in that church except what this little controlling group decided should happen. The church had become their property; it belonged to them. After my investigation, I responded to the letter by saying that, under those circumstances, I felt no freedom in recommending a candidate for their pulpit.

This brings us to a further insight into what Jesus meant when he used the word *church*. He said, "I will build *my* church." The church Christ is building is *his*. It does not belong to the people, the members; they belong to him. It does not belong to the officers; they belong to him. It does not belong to the pastors; they belong to him. It does not belong to a hierarchy; the hierarchy belongs to him.

The church belongs to Jesus Christ. It does not belong to popes or presidents. It does not belong to committees. It does not belong to associations or agencies. It does not belong to a few people who move into positions of power in a local congregation and try to dictate whatever happens. *Whatever the church is, it belongs to Jesus Christ alone.*

Too Much Power

Sometimes I wonder if, millennia ago, God did not anticipate the condition of the contemporary church. The story of his judgment on Babel, recorded in the eleventh chapter of Genesis, sounds so familiar.

"Now the whole world had one language and a common speech. As men moved eastward, they found a plain in Shinar and settled there. They said to each other, 'Come, let's make bricks and bake them thoroughly.' They used brick instead of stone, and tar for mortar. Then they said, 'Come, let us build ourselves a city, with a tower that reaches to the heavens, so that we may make a name for ourselves and not be scattered over the face of the whole earth' " (verses 1-4).

The record continues, "The LORD said, 'If as one people speaking the same language they have begun to do this, then nothing they plan to do will be impossible for them' " (verse 6). Here we see an almost perfect sociological situation. One language, no linguistic barriers, no possibility of losing the meaning in translation. Think of the problems that linguistic differences have introduced into history! But these people would have no such problems, and nothing would be impossible for them.

God, however, did not think the situation was good. "Come, let us go down and confuse their language so they will not understand each other," he said. And as soon as the people could no longer understand one another, they abandoned their ambitious project. "The LORD scattered them from there over all the earth, and they stopped building the city" (verse 8).

Frustrated for Our Own Good

What evil did God see in their unity of language? What evil did he see in the fact that anything human beings wanted to do was possible for them?

Paul makes an interesting statement in one of his remarkable overviews of history, recorded in the eighth chapter of Romans. In verse 20 he comments, "The creation was subjected to frustration, not by its own choice, but by the will of the one who subjected it."

Is it possible that Paul's comment could be a commentary on the Babel story in Genesis 11? Why would God introduce frustration into human history by his sovereign act? Why is frustration at the heart of human history? Why did not God leave us in that beautiful condition of speaking one language, able to do anything we set our minds to?

Is it conceivable that God saw man's self-destruction in his own progress? Think of our advances in technology and science, in medicine, in psychology and psychiatry; in understanding how the brain functions, how our physical environment preserves life, how individuals communicate in family systems, how children learn. Think of the growth in entrepreneurial skills producing the large corporations of today, the advances in advertising and financing. With all this progress, have we solved the problems of disease, homelessness, and poverty? Are people happier? Are families stronger? Have morals improved? Are crime rates dropping? Is our educational system improving? Is the world closer to peace? Are we taking good care of our planet?

How much has all our progress improved the United States, or the world, during the last few centuries? Is it possible that God knows that if he left us with one language and limitless power, if nothing we planned to do was impossible for us, we would destroy ourselves almost immediately?

Who's in Charge?

Today many of us act as if we are responsible for building Christ's church. We have adopted the world's route to success. In building the church, we have become entrepreneurs, CEOs of great corporations. We use contemporary methods of advertising and promotion and marketing. We do market research and adapt our programs to meet the "felt needs" of the geographical area we have designated as our own. In short, we operate just as the world does, adapting as much as possible to the culture around us.

Is it possible that, millennia ago, God saw in Babel the cancer of bureaucracy, the uncontrolled growth of paperwork, committees, administrators, decision-making bodies? Organization is not evil; in fact, it is necessary. But too often it becomes an end in itself. Whether it takes the form of government bureaucracy or church hierarchy, it begins to perpetuate itself, to own what it was intended to serve. And as soon as an organization does that, it loses touch with the people. When this happens in the church, it also loses touch with Jesus Christ.

The church does not belong to its leaders. It belongs to Jesus. It is his property. And all who are a part of the church he is building are his. They belong to him, and they are to serve his will, his purpose in history.

Desperately we need to recover this reality, this fact about the church Christ is building. The church is a living organism, not just an organization. Christ is its head, and he alone is in charge.

Note

1. Oswald Chambers, *My Utmost for His Highest* (Westwood, N.J.: Barbour and Company, Ltd., 1963).

Chapter Three

Invincible and Indestructible

The light shines in the darkness, and the darkness did
not overcome it.

John 1:5 (NRSV)

In response to Peter's testimony, Jesus said, "On
this rock I will build my church, and the gates of
Hades will not overcome it" (Matthew 16:18).
The church, as Jesus used the term, is something he
is building. It belongs to him. And it is indestructible and invincible. As the King James Version puts
it, "the gates of hell shall not prevail against it."

Jesus' promise implies that the church will be
active in its confrontation with evil. Gates are not
offensive weapons. They protect the fortress. They
are defensive. Apparently when Jesus used the word
church, he was thinking of the force that would
oppose evil in history, actively and victoriously.

In other words, the church does not capitulate to evil lying down. Neither is the church reactionary. Instead, the church that Jesus Christ described is a moral force in the world against evil. It is not passive; it is dynamic. It assaults the gates of hell. It confronts evil. It does not give in!

The Church's Dwindling Influence

In recent years we have seen a strange and disappointing contradiction. Despite the resurgence of evangelicalism—its visibility in the press and in other media, the incredible growth of television ministries touching the lives of millions, and the unprecedented involvement of the evangelical community in the political process—there seems to have been no corresponding influence on the United States social order. While evangelicalism has prospered, our culture has decayed. Social evils have been increasing epidemically. The world has been made aware of evangelicalism as perhaps at no other time in American history, and yet it has not been a force for righteousness and justice in the nation in any measurable way.

Yes, there are grand exceptions to my pessimistic assessment, for which we can praise God. But while the evangelical voice has grown loud and powerful, the incidence of divorce, battered wives, child abuse, permissive sex, alcohol and drug abuse, pornography, and homosexuality have increased. Evangelicals have taken positions against these evils, but why has the evangelical church not been battering the gates of hell in the name of truth, justice, and righteousness? Could it be that our lack of moral force in society today is due to the fact that the evangelical community has been infected and corrupted by these same social evils?

The popularity of the so-called health-and-wealth gospel has somehow emasculated the church, making it impotent. Great numbers of evangelicals, despite their vocal testimony for Christ, seem to be quite comfortable and happy and content in the materialism of this age. This certainly is not the product of God's building.

In the prologue to his Gospel, John writes, "The light shines in the darkness; and the darkness has not overcome it" (John 1:5, NRSV). Darkness has no power over light. It cannot snuff it out or extinguish it. The power is all with the light. Jesus said to his disciples, "You are the light of the world" (Matthew 5:14). Somehow that light must be hidden in our contemporary world, for it does not seem as if the church is mounting successful assaults against the gates of hell.

Trouble from the World

The church Christ is building is not only invincible; it is indestructible. Every effort that the world has ever made to destroy the church has only resulted in strengthening it and causing it to grow. Persecution in Jerusalem under Saul of Tarsus in the days of the apostles served to scatter the church and spread the message abroad. So it has been throughout the ages. Adversity, resistance, opposition, and even persecution have not only failed to destroy the church; they have caused the church to increase in numbers and grow stronger than ever.

Jesus told his disciples that his church would have trouble in the world. He said, "If the world hates you, keep in mind that it hated me first. . . . If they persecuted me, they will persecute you also" (John

15:18, 20). "In this world you will have trouble," Jesus said. "But take heart! I have overcome the world" (John 16:33).

The church Christ is building is hated by the world. The church Christ is building is opposed by the world. The church Christ is building is mistreated by the world. But what of the church today? Apart from some grand and glorious exceptions, the church seeks acceptance by the world. It really enjoys its friendship with the world: it exploits it and panders to it.

It must have seemed that the church of Jesus Christ was defeated in China in 1949 when the pastors were imprisoned, the buildings confiscated, and the missionaries evicted. But the very opposite happened. In thirty years, under oppression, the church of Jesus Christ grew as it had not during the previous hundred years.

The reality of Christ's church—invincible and indestructible—has been proven over and over in Eastern Europe and the former Soviet Union with the total breakdown of communism. The church, forced underground for all practical purposes for the past seventy years, has now surfaced. This resurgence is exciting, but it is more than that: it shows that the church Christ is building cannot be destroyed by the powers of the world.

One Generation from Demise

In 1990 I was invited to speak at the anniversary celebration of Young Life at a great conference in San Diego. The same year I was invited to speak at commencement at three Christian colleges in the United States. In preparation for these opportunities,

I began to take a careful look at the condition of this generation of young people.

It has long been accepted as self-evident that any local congregation is only one generation away from its own demise. This statement recognizes that the children and youth of a community of faith are the future of that community. If they leave, the community will die. That is why the church must take its young people seriously. They must be given the best possible education, discipleship, and training.

Today we are facing a crisis with regard to our young people. Middle-aged and older people always say that things aren't what they used to be. This time, they are right. Look at this paragraph from Chuck Miller's book, *Parenting the Adolescent* (Barnabas, Inc.: 1988):

"A 1940 survey of public school authorities found their top discipline problems were talking, gum chewing, making noise, running in the halls, getting out of turn in line, dressing improperly and littering. A 1986 poll of educators listed rape, robbery, assault, burglary, arson, bombings, murder, suicide, absenteeism, vandalism, drug abuse, alcohol abuse, gang warfare, pregnancy, abortion and venereal disease."

What has changed between 1940 and today? Why is this generation of young people different from earlier ones? My observations lead me to believe that this generation—unlike my children's generation or my own or my parents' or my grandparents'—is informed almost exclusively by its peers.

Leadership Needed Right Now

When I was a teenager, I do not remember talking about "peer pressure." Obviously my friends in school had a tremendous influence on me, but my family, my community, and my schools had a remarkable influence as well. If I got out of line, a neighbor would deal with me and then see to it that my parents knew about it. If it involved lawbreaking, they would not take me to the police station. They would take me home and talk to my parents about it. When I was in elementary and junior high school, I can remember dreaded visits to the principal's office. Not only did such visits mean a severe scolding from somebody held in great respect by the student body; they also often involved what we called "the rubber hose," a length of garden hose applied with some energy to my bottom. Though my peers had a great influence on my life, it did not compare to the influence of my home, neighborhood, and educators.

Today, as I see it, most of these influences are gone. We hear a great deal about the dysfunctional family. Neighbors do not know each other, and communities and schools are often intimidated by the young people. In contemplating this situation, I began to realize that, if this generation is going to be saved, it is up to this generation to save it. We can't wait for some future leaders to come along and influence the world for good. If leadership is not exerted right now, this generation of youth will have no future to speak of.

Holiness Unto the Lord

In the providence of God I was asked to speak at the one hundredth anniversary of Asbury College in Kentucky. Arriving mid-afternoon, I was taken to dinner by the president in a lovely restaurant in a restored community near the college town, following which we went to the evening meeting. The meeting had just started when we entered the auditorium foyer, and the congregation was singing "A Mighty Fortress Is Our God."

As I entered the auditorium, I became aware of the inscription high on the wall above the platform: "Holiness Unto the Lord." I knew the strong Christian reputation of the college, but I had never seen those words engraved over the platform in a college campus auditorium. The music of a choir of two hundred, together with an orchestra and the congregation, was absolutely thrilling, but my attention was gripped even more by that inscription: "Holiness Unto the Lord." It seemed to me to be God's answer to this generation of youth who profess faith in Christ, if they are going to save their own generation.

The following morning as I faced that great convocation of college young people, I asked if they would join me in singing the hymn, "Holy, Holy, Holy." As we sang, I turned my back to them and gazed again at those glorious words above the platform. When we finished the hymn, I turned and faced the young people, standing quietly for a moment. Then I said, " 'Holiness Unto the Lord.' Every time you enter this auditorium you see those words. Or do you? Is it possible that familiarity with those words, because you see them so often, has caused them to be, for all practical effects, erased from the wall?"

My message to that convocation, to the Young Life celebration, and to the three commencements at which I spoke was the same: "Holiness Unto the Lord." How desperately we need to recover this theme! Even in the holiest of churches, this generation of youth desperately needs to see holiness. Not superficial piety, but authentic Godlikeness, Christlikeness, in the lives of their peers. Holiness is what the whole world needs to see. All generations desperately need to see a holy people when they look at the church.

A Clean Break with the World

Tragic as was the TV scandal involving P.T.L., with the ensuing confusion and hostility among TV personalities, two positive results have come from it. First, the materialism that has so badly infected the evangelical community, especially some of the television ministries and their loyal supporters, has been exposed. Second, it has become clear, through media delight in exploiting this aberration of Christianity, that the world has no idea of what biblical faith is all about.

These two results from the negative scenario may turn out to benefit the evangelical community, if they awaken the church to the insidious way in which it has been encultured by the world around it. May God grant that the church will open its eyes, learn to distinguish itself from the world, and break decisively from the materialism that has made it so comfortable and acceptable in our secularist society. The church needs to learn, generation by generation, that "friendship with the world is hatred toward God" (James 4:4).

Certainly it is obvious that the invincibility of the church, its indestructibility, does not depend upon conformity to the world around it. The very opposite is true: the invincibility, the indestructibility, the power of the church Christ is building is based upon the fact that it is *utterly other* than the life around it in the culture around it. The life of the church is supernatural. It is the life of God in Christ manifesting itself in the bodies of believers wherever they are. "It is the power of God for the salvation of everyone who believes" (Romans 1:16).

A Supernatural Life

Nothing is clearer in the Bible than the fact that the life of the believer is a supernatural life. It is literally the life of God in Christ in the believer. This was the message of Pentecost. This is fundamental to understanding the nature of the church that Christ is building. As the Father "clothed" himself in the body of the Jewish carpenter, his Son, in order to manifest himself to the world, so the Father, in Christ, clothes himself with the bodies of believers. Wherever and whenever believers meet together in Christ's name, the life of God is made manifest by the power of the Holy Spirit. As Jesus said to his disciples, "Where two or three come together in my name, there am I with them" (Matthew 18:20). This life is invincible. This life is indestructible.

Nothing is clearer in the New Testament than the fact that the pilgrimage with Christ is one of allowing Christ to live his life, to manifest his will and his love and his good pleasure, in the life of the believers by the power of the Holy Spirit. The believer has no life except the life of Christ. This is the significance of Paul's statement to the Galatians: "I have been crucified with Christ and I no longer live, but Christ lives in me. The life I live in the body, I live by faith in the Son of God, who loved me and gave himself for me" (Galatians 2:20).

The believer is buried with Christ in baptism and raised with Christ in resurrection (see Romans 6:4). The life that is in the believer is the life of Christ. This is antithetical to the ways of the world. This doesn't make any sense to the world. It is contrary to the wisdom of the world which, incidentally, the apostle Paul says is "foolishness in God's sight" (1 Corinthians 3:19).

The Power of Christ in You

In writing to the Colossians, Paul speaks about his mission in history. God gave him the commission "to present to you the word of God in its fullness—the mystery that has been kept hidden for ages and generations, but is now disclosed to the saints" (Colossians 1:25, 26). This mystery, he says, is "Christ in you, the hope of glory" (verse 27). Notice that he did not say that Christ is the hope of glory. He said that Christ *in you* is the hope of glory.

The believer is one in whom Christ dwells. The believer is one whose body is the habitation of Christ. The church that Christ is building confronts the world, not by cleverness or wisdom, not by programs or methods or institutions. The church Christ is building confronts the world in the very power of God himself in the life of the believer.

The church that Christ is building is an organism of which Christ is the head and of which Christ is the life. The church is invincible and indestructible against this world only when it manifests this life of Christ. It certainly is not invincible with its programs, its methods, its seminars. The church has no impact on the world when it uses the world's ways of influencing the world. As someone put it, "The church is the most influential in the world when it is at its most other worldly."

There is no human force or wisdom, organization or program on earth that can destroy Satan and his determination to be victorious in history. The power of God alone can confront the gates of hell and not be destroyed by them. The power of Christ alone, in his believers, can make his church indestructible and invincible.

Chapter Four

The Keys to the Kingdom

I will give you the keys of the kingdom of heaven; whatever you bind on earth will be bound in heaven, and whatever you loose on earth will be loosed in heaven.

Matthew 16:19

One penetrating insight into the church Christ is building comes from our Lord's statement to Peter following his great confession. "I will give you the keys of the kingdom of heaven," Jesus said; "whatever you bind on earth will be bound in heaven, and whatever you loose on earth will be loosed in heaven" (Matthew 16:19).

The Roman Catholic church is unequivocal in its interpretation of this statement: The keys to the kingdom represent the authority invested in the church over the resources of grace. Traditionally Catholics have taught that this authority resides with the Roman church hierarchy. Protestants, of course, do not accept this view, and yet one rarely hears Protestants talk about this simple passage of Scripture at all.

The Authority of Agreement

Fortunately, in a totally different context, Jesus makes a similar statement without referring to the keys of the kingdom. It is a passage worth studying. Not only does it clarify what Jesus meant when he spoke to Peter; it also gives insights about the church on which Catholics and Protestants can agree.

In Matthew 18:18 Jesus repeats, "I tell you the truth, whatever you bind on earth will be bound in heaven, and whatever you loose on earth will be loosed in heaven."

As if that were not astounding enough, Jesus compounds our amazement as he promises, "Again, I tell you that if two of you on earth agree about anything you ask for, it will be done for you by my Father in heaven" (verse 19).

Talk about the keys to the kingdom! Jesus promises incredible authority based upon one simple condition—agreement. It is clear in the context that this agreement is not one that is negotiated through discussion and debate. It is, rather, the consensus that comes through finding the will of God in the mind of Christ. As a matter of fact, that remarkable promise is connected to Jesus' next statement with the conjunction *for:* "For where two or three come together in my name, there am I with them" (verse 20).

Paul exhorted the Philippian believers to "let this mind be in you, which was also in Christ Jesus" (2:5, KJV). In another context he declared, "We have the mind of Christ" (1 Corinthians 2:16). It seems clear that what Jesus is saying is that when two or more come together in his name, he is with them, and there is a real prospect of finding his will through consensus. This grants the church incredible authority in heaven.

The Mind of Christ

The mind of Christ is the key. God's thinking and human thinking are antithetical. Isaiah is explicit about this when he proclaims God's words: " 'For my thoughts are not your thoughts, neither are your ways my ways,' declares the LORD. 'As the heavens are higher than the earth, so are my ways higher than your ways and my thoughts than your thoughts' " (Isaiah 55:8, 9). When we humans think our best thoughts and go our best ways, we are actually contrary to God's thoughts and God's ways.

The apostle Paul certainly understood this reality. He wrote to the church at Corinth:

"When I came to you, brothers, I did not come with eloquence or superior wisdom as I proclaimed to you the testimony about God. For I resolved to know nothing while I was with you except Jesus Christ and him crucified. I came to you in weakness and fear, and with much trembling. My message and my preaching were not with wise and persuasive words, but with a demonstration of the Spirit's power, so that your faith might not rest on men's wisdom, but on God's power" (1 Corinthians 2:1-5).

Preceding this statement the apostle had said, "The foolishness of God is wiser than man's wisdom, and the weakness of God is stronger than man's strength" (1:25). The power and authority of the church Christ is building comes not from decisions made individually or corporately by the church, not by majority rule, but when the church seeks the mind of Christ and when it speaks that mind. Then, and only then, it has his power and his authority.

A Reconciled Community

Jesus' remarkable promise is prefaced by an important condition that can be stated in one word: *reconciliation:*

"If your brother sins against you, go and show him his fault, just between the two of you. If he listens to you, you have won your brother over. But if he will not listen, take one or two others along, so that 'every matter may be established by the testimony of two or three witnesses.' If he refuses to listen to them, tell it to the church; and if he refuses to listen even to the church, treat him as you would a pagan or a tax collector" (Matthew 18:15-17).

The people of God are under orders to deal with alienation in the community. Whether one is the offended (Matthew 18:15) or the offender (Matthew 5:23-24), a Christian is to take the initiative in being reconciled. It should be expected that the message of reconciliation, so far as the world is concerned, is meaningless if brothers and sisters in Christ are unable to maintain their own relationships in peace and harmony. But Christians who are reconciled with one another show the world what reconciliation means.

In other words, to put it in the New Testament way, they are a *fellowship*. As John wrote in his first epistle, "We proclaim to you what we have seen and heard, so that you also may have fellowship with us.

And our fellowship is with the Father and with his Son, Jesus Christ" (1 John 1:3). Alienation in the church is intolerable. It renders the church impotent. Reconciliation empowers the church. It is what redemption is all about.

A Reconciling Community

The church that Christ is building is a reconciled community, committed to reconciling the world to God and to each other. In Paul's words to the church at Corinth:

"Therefore, if anyone is in Christ, he is a new creation; the old has gone, the new has come! All this is from God, who reconciled us to himself through Christ and gave us the ministry of reconciliation: that God was reconciling the world to himself in Christ, not counting men's sins against them. And he has committed to us the message of reconciliation. We are therefore Christ's ambassadors, as though God were making his appeal through us. We implore you on Christ's behalf: Be reconciled to God. God made him who had no sin to be sin for us, so that in him we might become the righteousness of God" (2 Corinthians 5:17-21).

Our self-alienation from God is the root of sin; reconciliation with God through the life, death, and resurrection of Jesus Christ is the gospel, the good news. The message of reconciliation is that "God was reconciling the world to himself in Christ." The ministry of reconciliation is the work God has given to his church: those who have been reconciled to God through Christ should be his ambassadors in the world, reconciling the world to God.

The church Christ is building is a reconciled and

reconciling community. Obviously it will have no reconciling force if it is alienated within itself.

Reconciliation Has Priority

In the Sermon on the Mount Jesus twice made this very clear: that reconciliation has priority over everything else. In the fifth chapter of Matthew, Jesus said, "If you are offering your gift at the altar and there remember that your brother has something against you, leave your gift there in front of the altar. First go and be reconciled to your brother; then come and offer your gift" (verses 23, 24). Reconciliation has priority over worship. We are not ready to worship God if we are alienated from a brother or sister in Christ. Worship must be based on fellowship, for "love is the fulfillment of the law" (Romans 13:10).

In the sixth chapter of Matthew, after teaching what we call the Lord's prayer, Jesus lifted from it one petition as if to say, "This is fundamental to prayer": "If you forgive men when they sin against you, your heavenly Father will also forgive you. But if you do not forgive men their sins, your Father will not forgive your sins" (verses 14, 15). The forgiven person is a forgiving person. The unforgiving person is not in a position to be forgiven. Alienation should be treated as intolerable in the servant of Jesus Christ, for alienation renders the individual, and the whole church, powerless.

Love, a Sign of Discipleship

Following the institution of the Lord's Supper as it is recorded in the thirteenth chapter of John's Gospel, Jesus washed his disciples' feet and urged them to do likewise. He said to them, "A new command I give you: Love one another. As I have loved you, so you must love one another." He added, "All men will know that you are my disciples, if you love one another" (John 13:34, 35). Our discipleship is manifested by our love, one for the other.

The high priestly prayer of our Lord Jesus Christ, which he prayed shortly before his arrest and trials, is recorded in the seventeenth chapter of John's Gospel. At the heart of that prayer, Jesus prays for the unity of believers, not only the twelve disciples and the church of their time, but also all those who would believe in Jesus through them. Jesus said,

"My prayer is not for them alone. I pray also for those who will believe in me through their message, that all of them may be one, Father, just as you are in me and I am in you. May they also be in us so that the world may believe that you have sent me. . . . May they be brought to complete unity to let the world know that you sent me and have loved them even as you have loved me" (John 17:20, 21, 23).

This is just another way of saying that the church Christ is building is a reconciled and a reconciling community. It is a community of love—love for God and love for others as well as love for self.

The Importance of Fellowship

Luke records a significant fact about the apostolic church fresh from its Pentecost experience. He described the church thus: "They devoted themselves to the apostles' teaching and to the fellowship, to the breaking of bread and to prayer" (Acts 2:42). Apparently the disciples' fellowship—that is, the relationship they had with Jesus Christ and with each other, which was a learning experience for them during his time on earth with them—was seen as very important. Fellowship, in fact, was as important as Scripture ("the apostles' teaching") or sacrament ("the breaking of bread") or worship ("prayer").

The rest of the second chapter of Acts describes the beautiful relationships that developed among the early believers. They were a community. They were generous to those in need. They worshiped and ate and praised God together. And people were attracted to them because they were a reconciled and a reconciling community, a community of love, a community of people who cared for each other.

In contemporary evangelicalism, fellowship has been devalued. It has come to mean having a cup of coffee after church in the social hall, or gathering for a potluck supper. In fact, many churches call their multipurpose room "Fellowship Hall." Fellowship, as we understand it in the contemporary church, is reserved for a brief time with one another after we worship and before we disperse for other activities.

Too often we see fellowship as incidental and peripheral to the life of the church. Doctrine or Scripture study or the sermon seem much more important, as do prayer and the sacraments. Not so in the apostolic church. The believers' fellowship was treated with equal importance to doctrine, the breaking of bread, and prayer. Fellowship was taken seriously.

Love, the Key to the Kingdom

When asked what is the greatest commandment, Jesus answered immediately, " 'Love the Lord your

God with all your heart and with all your soul and with all your mind.' This is the first and greatest commandment. And the second is like it: 'Love your neighbor as yourself.' All the Law and the Prophets hang on these two commandments" (Matthew 22:37-39).

The apostle Paul declared that the law is fulfilled in one word, love (Romans 13:10). In the fourth chapter of his first Epistle, John urges us to love one another: "Dear friends, let us love one another, for love comes from God. Everyone who loves has been born of God and knows God. Whoever does not love does not know God, because God is love" (verses 7, 8). The reasonableness of John's exhortation is simply beyond dispute. The one who is born again loves; the one who does not love, does not know God. John concludes: "If anyone says, 'I love God,' yet hates his brother, he is a liar. For anyone who does not love his brother, whom he has seen, cannot love God, whom he has not seen" (verse 20). Very strong language, but it is a word from the Lord. It repudiates every effort to devalue love.

The greatest force in history is love—the love of God, agape love, love that is unconditional. This kind of love is not emotional, sentimental, a matter of feeling only; it is volitional. It is a decision to love, to obey God's command to love, to be an instrument of his unconditional love. This is the church Christ is building—a church that loves as God loves.

Fellowship is the key to authority and power in Christ's church. Broken relationships, discord, and alienation render the church without authority in heaven or on earth. But when believers gather together in one mind—the mind of Christ—whatever they bind on earth will be bound in heaven, and whatever they loose on earth will be loosed in heaven. Reconciled and reconciling, in fellowship with God and with one another, they will have the keys of the kingdom.

Chapter Five

A Living Fellowship

We proclaim to you what we have seen and heard, so that you also may have fellowship with us. And our fellowship is with the Father and with his Son, Jesus Christ.

1 John 1:3

Jesus was committed to a ministry that was universal in prospect. He was going to start a movement that would reach the whole world and last forever, and he had three years in which to do it. What was his strategy?

He chose twelve men to be with him. He did not neglect the multitudes: he loved them, taught them, fed them, healed them, made himself always available to them. But he devoted himself to the twelve men. And, incidentally, he knew what was in the hearts of those twelve men. He knew that Judas would betray him. He knew that Peter would deny him. He knew that all but John would abandon him at the cross. But before his ascension he left with these twelve men, save one, the responsibility for the mission to which he had been called and for which he had given his life—the mission to reach the world.

That They Might Be with Him

Mark, in the third chapter of his Gospel, records that Jesus "appointed twelve—designating them apostles—that they might be with him and that he might send them out to preach and to have authority to drive out demons" (verses 14, 15). The preposition *with* is a big word in that passage: "that they might be *with* him." It is a big word in understanding the ministry of Jesus Christ and in understanding what it means to be a discipler of people. It conveys Jesus' love, his desire for fellowship.

Perhaps the word *with* can be best understood in the context of Jesus' remarkable promise, "I am with you always, to the very end of the age" (Matthew 28:20). Jesus promised never to leave us or forsake us. This is the same promise, incidentally, that God made to Joshua after Moses' death, just before Joshua led the children of Israel across the Jordan into the promised land (see Joshua 1:5).

The "withness" of God is one of life's most precious realities. We are never alone, not even in death: "Even though I walk through the valley of the shadow of death, I will fear no evil, for you are with me" (Psalm 23:4). We are never forsaken, never forgotten, never left out. In the New Testament, *with* means a permanent, enduring, indeed eternal relationship. God came to us in

Christ, "Immanuel—which means, 'God with us'" (Matthew 1:23).

The fact that God is with us cannot be exaggerated or overstated. It is at the heart of understanding the church Christ is building. It is of the essence of the community of faith. Once again we return to Jesus' promise, this time with a new emphasis: "Where two or three come together in my name, there am I *with* them" (Matthew 18:20, emphasis added).

No Agenda But Love

If we take Jesus seriously and make him our model for discipleship, then we do not need a book or a workshop or a class on how to disciple. What we need is to make a decision: to choose to be *with* the person we are called to disciple. We cannot disciple someone through a book or through television. We cannot disciple in absentia. We can disciple only as Jesus did, by being with the one discipled. It is a costly endeavor. It takes time and effort. It is much simpler to write a letter or give someone a book or lay down a set of precepts for the person to follow. But if we take discipling seriously, there is simply no substitute for *withness*.

As we study the Gospel record of Jesus' life and the contacts he made with people, whether singly or in groups, we begin to realize that he had no agenda except that which love dictated when he was with a person. He never treated any two people in the same way, never responded in a set manner. In other words, he did not have a single "method" by which he operated. He treated each person differently according to that person's need at the moment.

To the rich young ruler he said, "Go, sell your

possessions and give to the poor, and you will have treasure in heaven. Then come, follow me" (Matthew 19:21).

To Zacchaeus he said, "Come down immediately. I must stay at your house today" (Luke 19:5).

To the woman at the well in Samaria he said, "Will you give me a drink?" (John 4:7).

To Nicodemus, the Pharisee, he said, "No one can see the kingdom of God unless he is born again" (John 3:3).

Every person he addressed, every involvement he had, was different from all the others, so it is impossible to say "this is the way" Jesus discipled people. He did not have an agenda or a method—except love!

No Substitute for "Withness"

To digress for a moment, when I look back upon my early pilgrimage with Christ—my zeal, my aggressiveness in wanting to win everybody to Christ—I wonder how many more I alienated from him than I won to him. I had an agenda. It was a good agenda. It was evangelism, and therefore I thought it was justifiable.

As I approached people, their circumstances were not important to me. I wanted to get them to accept Christ as quickly as possible, and I did not have time to listen to them, to hear them, to ask them questions, to learn about their needs or situation. My agenda, evangelism, was paramount. It took priority over all the needs and circumstances of the people that I was to win for Christ.

Now, many years later, I am not ashamed of that zeal, but I wish that my enthusiasm had been more loving, more tender, more understanding. I wish I had been more concerned about the ones to whom I was speaking.

We don't really get to know people by corresponding with them or visiting them occasionally. The only way we really get to know someone is by being with him or her. This fact is so clear to me at my age. After fifty-one years of marriage, there is no way to describe verbally what I feel with my wife and what I believe she feels with me. There is no substitute for "withness" in marriage, in the family, in friendships, in evangelism, in discipleship. "With" is the big word.

The Presence of Jesus

Try to imagine what it must have been like to be with Jesus during those three years of his ministry on earth. It would not have been a formal course of discipleship. His disciples learned and grew just by hearing what he said and seeing what he did. Most importantly, perhaps, they were with him nearly every day.

How wonderful the presence of this man Jesus must have been! How secure his disciples must have felt with him! We can appreciate the importance of their being with Jesus when we look at the Gospel stories about what happened when Jesus deliberately departed from them for a period of time.

For example, the sixth chapter of Mark tells about one time when the disciples were alone in a boat:

"When evening came, the boat was in the middle

of the lake, and [Jesus] was alone on land. He saw the disciples straining at the oars, because the wind was against them. About the fourth watch of the night he went out to them, walking on the lake. He was about to pass by them, but when they saw him walking on the lake, they thought he was a ghost. They cried out, because they all saw him and were terrified" (verses 47-50).

Without Jesus, the disciples were fatigued by the prevailing wind. They were frightened by the unknown. Only when Jesus called out to them—"Take courage! It is I. Don't be afraid"—and joined them in the boat were their fears relieved. Only when Jesus was with them did the wind die down.

Just to Be with You

Mark 3:14 became a vital text in my ministry. Jesus "appointed twelve . . . that they might be with him." As my ministry developed through the years, I came to the point of defining it as "being with someone at his or her convenience in terms of time and place, without an agenda." Let me describe one of my first experiences in following this ministry.

It was in the mid to late forties, and I was new on the staff of First Presbyterian Church of Hollywood. I had been called to shepherd, or disciple, men (incidentally, we didn't use the word *disciple* as a verb in those days). I had begun this ministry in the small town of Coalinga, where I had pastored for three years. But I found that in the great metropolitan area of Los Angeles, I was unable to contact men.

I decided how I would operate. I would prayerfully look over the congregation on Sunday morning or

Sunday evening as I was assisting in the service, and I would trust the Spirit to direct me to the one I would contact to be with that week.

The first time I did this, I approached the one I sensed God was leading me to as soon as the benediction was over. I asked him if I could spend some time with him that week. He invited me to be his guest for lunch at his downtown club.

On Tuesday I met him at his club at 12:30. We had a delightful lunch and a good conversation. At about twenty minutes to two he looked at his watch and said, "Dick, I have a two o'clock appointment in my office. I have only ten minutes left. What did you want?"

I said, "I didn't want anything. I just wanted to be with you."

He responded, "Come on, Halverson, I know preachers! You want something. You want me to do something for the church. You need some money."

"No," I said, "honestly, I just wanted to be with you."

He was silent for what seemed a long time, and then he said this: "Dick, this is the first time I've been with a preacher when he didn't want something from me."

Ministry without People

Think about that. Think what we unintentionally communicate to those we are supposed to love and win and disciple. Isn't it tragic to think that all the while we are with them, they assume we have a hidden agenda that will sooner or later be made manifest? And they are not even able to hear what we say in the process, because they are waiting for us to tell them why we really want to be with them.

Almost every time I have spoken at a preachers' retreat, seminar, or conference and mentioned this way of ministering to which God has led me, many say to me, "But Dick, I just don't have the time." To me, this is a commentary on where we put our priorities in the pastorate these days. No time for people, no time for their needs, no time for their hurts, no time for their tragedies.

A ministry that has no time for people is the very antithesis of Jesus' ministry, the antithesis of his way of love, the antithesis of his way of discipling. And yet so many contemporary pastors are preoccupied with the business of inventing, promoting, administering, and perpetuating programs, organizations, and property.

Building, Body, and Bride

The apostle Paul uses three analogies for the church. In understanding them, we may have a clearer understanding of the word *fellowship* as the New Testament uses it. The church is like a *building*. The church is like a body. The church is like a *bride*.

These three analogies have one thing in common. In each case, relationships are fundamental.

In a building, the rooms, doors, windows, floors, ceilings, pipes, electrical circuits, and all the other parts must relate to one another, or the building will be unusable. In addition, all the parts must relate to the building as a whole, both in appearance and in function, or the building will be a curiosity or an eyesore.

In the body, the members must be rightly related to one another, or the body will be dysfunctional, crippled, or ill. The members must also be rightly related to the head, or they will be unable to carry out their tasks.

In marriage, everything depends upon the relationship of the bride to the groom, and of the groom to the bride. No matter what else a husband and wife have, if they are not rightly related to each other, their marriage is a failure.

Fellowship Leads to Fruitfulness

The apostle John, one of the founding members of that early church, tells us that fellowship is the consummate end of God's redemptive purpose in history: "We proclaim to you what we have seen and heard, so that you also may have fellowship with us. And our fellowship is with the Father and with his Son, Jesus Christ" (1 John 1:3). The witness to Jesus Christ in the world is a witness to fellowship. Or, to look at the matter conversely, no matter what the church says and does in its attempt to witness to the world, if it does not demonstrate authentic New Testament fellowship, its witness is not bearing fruit as it ought.

Fellowship leads to fruitfulness. We see this clearly in Luke's description of the apostolic community. The last sentence in that chapter, which sounds almost like an afterthought or a footnote, is this: "And the Lord added to their number daily those who were being saved" (Acts 2:47).

The significance of that simple sentence is overwhelming. Contemplate the spontaneity, the sheer effortlessness of evangelism in the apostolic community! The point is this: when relationships are right in the fellowship of faith, evangelism is automatic. It happens all the time.

When we consider the time and effort spent by today's church organizing programs and seminars and workshops, developing textbooks and how-to books and videos on evangelism, teaching leaders about motivation and marketing and learning methods—we can see how far we have come from the apostolic community, and how desperately we need to be taken back two thousand years.

Authentic Church Growth

This brings us to the matter of church growth. Time after time, when I am invited to speak to church or pastors' groups, I begin by saying, "I'm going to give you two words, and I want you to tell me the first thing you think of when you hear these two words." Then I say, "Church growth."

Invariably—and there has never been an exception to this—those who respond say they think immediately of numbers or additions. No one has ever suggested that church growth has to do with growing "in the grace and knowledge of our Lord and Savior Jesus Christ" (2 Peter 3:18). No one has ever mentioned that it has to do with growing in our relationships with one another in Christ.

Yet that's where the emphasis was in the apostolic community. They grew by the infilling of the Holy Spirit in their relationships with one another and with Jesus. They lived authentic New Testament fellowship—a fact, by the way, that caused them to enjoy "the favor of all the people" (Acts 2:47). And the Lord brought new believers to them daily.

Growth into Christ

Keeping church growth in mind, examine Paul's word to the Ephesians, chapter 4. Here we see authentic church growth. In verse 11 Paul lists the gifts Christ left the church when he ascended into heaven: "some to be apostles, some to be prophets, some to be evangelists, and some to be pastors and teachers." In verse 12, he tells the purpose of the gifts: "to prepare God's people for works of service, so that the body of Christ may be built up." And then he describes church growth as the New Testament understands it:

"We all reach unity in the faith and in the knowledge of the Son of God and become mature, attaining to the whole measure of the fullness of Christ. Then we will no longer be infants, tossed back and forth by the waves, and blown here and there by every wind of teaching. . . . Instead, speaking the truth in love, we will in all things *grow up into him who is the Head, that is, Christ.* From him the whole body, joined and held together by every supporting ligament, *grows and builds itself up in love,* as each part does its work" (Ephesians 4:13-16, emphasis added).

Again, in Colossians 2:18-19 Paul says:

"Do not let anyone who delights in false humility and the worship of angels disqualify you for the prize. Such a person . . . has lost connection with the Head, from whom the whole body, supported and held together by its ligaments and sinews, *grows as God causes it to grow* (emphasis added).

There is church growth in the New Testament— growth into Christ, growth in love, growth as God directs. Additions in membership are a result of that kind of growth. When the church is a living fellowship, Christ adds to it daily those who are being saved.

Chapter Six

Born of the Spirit

Do not leave Jerusalem, but wait for the gift my Father promised, which you have heard me speak about. For John baptized with water, but in a few days you will be baptized with the Holy Spirit.

Acts 1:4, 5

Once when Billy Graham was planning a city-wide crusade in the United States, a pastor is reported to have said in the planning meeting, "If we have this crusade here, Billy Graham will set the church back one hundred years."

When Billy heard this, he replied, "One hundred years! I want to set the church back two thousand years!"

By this he certainly did not mean he wants to abandon or forget or disregard two thousand years of church history and all that has happened since Christ was on earth. But he wants today's church to discover the secret of the apostolic community. What was the key to their incredible outreach—three thousand on the day of Pentecost, a continual influx of new believers day by day following that, and then just a little bit later, five thousand at once?

A Careful Historian

Providentially, it is unnecessary to speculate concerning the apostolic church. God has wonderfully provided us with a sacred record, written by a medical scientist, Luke, who was not only interested in historical accuracy, but was a master of the Greek language and used it with precision. Dr. Luke was trained in the tradition of Hippocrates, the name from whom we get the Hippocratic oath. Diagnosis is based on observation or the inductive method. He was trained to secure all the information possible about his patients, to examine carefully the symptoms in order to make an accurate diagnosis and prescribe an adequate cure. He gives us an insight into his dedication to these skills as he opens his Gospel:

"Many have undertaken to draw up an account of the things that have been fulfilled among us, just as they were handed down to us by those who from the first were eyewitnesses and servants of the word. Therefore, since I myself have carefully investigated everything from the beginning, it seemed good also to me to write an orderly account for you, most excellent Theophilus, so that you may know the certainty of the things you have been taught" (Luke 1:1-4).

Luke makes four significant points in this brief introduction to his Gospel. First, he examined eyewitnesses who were with Jesus from the beginning of his ministry. Second, he "carefully investigated everything from the beginning." Third, his purpose was "to write an orderly account" based upon the testimony of the eyewitnesses and his own observations in order that, fourth, those who read "may know the certainty of the things [they] have been taught." Luke's historical skills and commitment stand with those of the best historians of his time.

Guided by the Holy Spirit, who would lead the disciples into all truth and bring to their remembrance the things they had seen and heard during his public ministry (John 14:26; 16:13), Luke then recorded in the Book of Acts the profile we have been reading of the apostolic church fresh from the experience of Pentecost.

Wait in Jerusalem

Jesus had instructed his disciples carefully and in great detail about what would happen after his ascension. He anticipated their trauma at his death and burial. He knew they would treat this as final and find in him no further hope. He was aware that, though he had often discussed with them his bodily resurrection, they would not understand. Jesus prepared them with what has been called the "last discourse" or "upper room discourse" recorded in the Gospel of John, chapters 14 through 16.

Jesus urged his disciples not to be troubled by the events that would soon take place. He told them that he was going to leave them, but that he was going to come again. He promised that those who believed in him would do his works and even greater works, because he was going to his Father. He promised them a "Counselor," in some versions called a "Comforter," the Holy Spirit, who would be *with* them and *in* them. He promised that he and his Father would come to the disciples and make their home with them.

Luke opens the Book of Acts by recording that Jesus commanded his followers, "Do not leave Jerusalem, but wait for the gift my Father promised, which you have heard me speak about" (Acts 1:4), in other words, the gift of the Holy Spirit. The disciples were to wait and do nothing until this promise was fulfilled. Indisputably, the promised gift of the Spirit would be fundamental, integral to all that would happen to Jesus' followers for all the future.

All Together in One Place

In the second chapter of Acts, Luke described the historic events of the day of Pentecost. He opens the chapter by stating two important facts. The first fact is this: "When the day of Pentecost came, they were all together in one place" (2:1).

What a beautiful picture of the unity of Christ's followers in obedience to his command! They had heard the promise Jesus had made in his last discourse. They knew that this promise came from God the Father, for Jesus had told them to wait for the gift his Father had promised. He had reminded them, "John baptized with water, but in a few days you will be baptized with the Holy Spirit" (1:5). Nevertheless, they probably were not too sure of the implications of this promise for themselves. They did not know what it meant.

In fact, the first question they asked Jesus after he had told them to wait in Jerusalem was this: "Lord, are you at this time going to restore the kingdom to

Israel?" (1:6). Obviously they were still thinking of Jesus as an earthly ruler, a conquering hero who would deal decisively with the Roman Empire. So Jesus told them explicitly what they were waiting for:

"You will receive power when the Holy Spirit comes on you; and you will be my witnesses in Jerusalem, and in all Judea and Samaria, and to the ends of the earth" (1:8).

The disciples, then, were waiting for this promise to be fulfilled. They were united in obedience and expectation. That is why "they were all together in one place."

Waiting for God's Time

Their togetherness is the first important fact Luke states in the second chapter of Acts. The second important fact is that they were together "when the day of Pentecost came" (2:1).

Pentecost was one of the major Jewish festivals. It commemorated the giving of the law at Sinai, and it was celebrated by bringing the first fruits to the Temple. Jesus' followers, all observant Jews, gathered in obedience to God to worship him as he directed.

Jesus had flatly refused to tell them when the Spirit would be given or the kingdom restored: "It is not for you to know the times or dates the Father has set by his own authority," he told them. It could have been the next day. It could have been years away. But they obeyed him and did not leave Jerusalem, did not forsake the practice of their Jewish religion.

God has a schedule. There is a *when* as well as a *what* to God's will. We are not really submitting to

God's will until we submit to the *when* as well as to the *what*, even—especially—if we do not know how long the wait will be. It may be just as wrong to say "Now" as to say "No" to God.

God's schedule often involves waiting. The Bible is full of stories about people who waited. Sarah waited for ninety years to give birth to her much-desired son, Isaac. The grieving Jacob waited for years in protracted mourning before learning his son, Joseph, was still alive. Joseph waited for years in prison before being elevated to the second-most important post in Pharaoh's government. Moses waited forty years in the wilderness to be prepared to lead Israel. Israel waited with the Red Sea in front of them and the Egyptian army in hot pursuit behind them until God miraculously opened the waters for them to pass through.

Waiting may be difficult, but it can be very good. "Be still before the LORD and wait patiently for him," says the psalmist (Psalm 37:7). Isaiah promises, "Those who wait for the LORD shall renew their strength, they shall mount up with wings like eagles, they shall run and not be weary, they shall walk and not faint" (Isaiah 40:31, NRSV).

The Birth of the Church

The disciples of Jesus Christ were waiting for God's schedule, a schedule they did not even know. But when God's promise was fulfilled on Pentecost, the fiftieth day after Passover, they had no doubts about what was happening. The gift was unmistakable.

That day there were signs, tremendous signs. "Suddenly a sound like the blowing of a violent wind came from heaven and filled the whole house where they were sitting. They saw what seemed to be tongues of fire that separated and came to rest on each of them. All of them were filled with the Holy Spirit and began to speak in other tongues as the Spirit enabled them" (Acts 2:2-4).

Here we see the birth of the church Christ is building.

It is important to distinguish between the signs and the substance of Pentecost, lest the signs be given greater significance than the reality. The signs—the sound of a violent wind, the tongues of fire, the speaking in other tongues—introduced history to this event, just as a heavenly choir and a star in the East introduced the world to the birth of Jesus. But the important fact that the signs pointed to was the coming of the Holy Spirit to the church, just as the important fact some thirty years earlier was the coming of God in human flesh to the earth. The substance was to continue, not necessarily the signs. The angelic choirs would return to heaven and the tongues of fire would fade, but the incarnate Christ and his indwelling Spirit would remain forever with humanity.

A Witness to the World

Luke records, "There were staying in Jerusalem Godfearing Jews from every nation under heaven" (2:5). When the multitude heard the sound of the rushing wind, when they heard the disciples speaking in many different languages, they "came together in bewilderment, because each one heard them speaking in his own language" (verse 6). Jesus had promised that through the gift of the Spirit, the disciples would witness to the entire world. Already the promise was being fulfilled, even before they set foot out of Jerusalem.

Devout Jews from every corner of the Roman Empire heard the witness of the Spirit-filled disciples speaking different languages, and they were amazed. "What does this mean?" some asked, while others said, "They have had too much wine" (verses 12, 13).

Rising to the challenge, Peter began to preach a powerful message. "What you are seeing is a fulfillment of prophecy," he said. "Jesus is risen from the dead. He is now sitting at God's right hand. What you are seeing and hearing is the work of his Holy Spirit. He is Lord, and he is the Messiah."

In response to Peter's sermon, three thousand people were baptized. They—and thousands of other Jews who had been in Jerusalem for the feast of Pentecost—would return to their own countries, bearing witness to what they had seen and heard. Within a few days of the birth of the Christian church, it already had thousands of missionaries, in every country of the world!

A Serving Community

The new Christians, says Luke, sold "their possessions and goods, [and] gave to anyone as he had need" (verse 45). The church Christ is building is a community of faith and love and obedience, a serving community that provides for its needy members. Luke reports:

"All the believers were one in heart and mind. No one claimed that any of his possessions was his own, but they shared everything they had. . . . There were no needy persons among them. For from time to time those who owned lands or houses sold them, brought the money from the sales and put it at the apostles' feet, and it was distributed to anyone as he had need" (Acts 4:32, 34, 35).

In the most natural way, the apostolic church knew that God is the owner and giver of all things. They correctly understood that we do not own anything; we simply hold it in trust from God. Under the constraint of love and justice, we use whatever God gives us to respond to those in need, to the glory of God.

It is important to point out that this generosity was not legislated. It was spontaneous. In fact, in the fifth chapter of Acts, Luke records the story of a man and his wife, Ananias and Sapphira, who sold a piece of property and kept back a portion of the selling price for themselves. When they gave some of the money to the apostles for distribution to the needy, Peter, inspired by the Holy Spirit, said, "How is it that Satan has so filled your heart that you have lied to the Holy Spirit and have kept for yourself some of the money you received for the land? Didn't it belong to you before it was sold? And after it was sold, wasn't the money at your disposal? What made you think of doing such a thing? You have not lied to men but to God" (Acts 5:3, 4).

The apostolic church did not require people to give up their possessions, but it took truth-telling very seriously. As a result of lying to the Holy Spirit, both Ananias and Sapphira dropped dead. Perhaps it is a commentary on the contemporary church that people no longer drop dead when they are caught in sin. Perhaps it means that today's church does not enjoy

the pristine purity of the apostolic church freshly
filled with the Holy Spirit and the love of God.

Concern for the Needy

In the last chapter we looked at a fact about that
apostolic community, the importance of which
simply cannot be exaggerated: "And the Lord added
to their number daily those who were being saved"
(2:47). We have looked at the four-point program of
the Spirit-filled apostolic church: the apostles'
teaching, fellowship, breaking of bread, and prayer.
Evangelism is not included in that program, and yet
evangelism was happening.

Evangelism occurred spontaneously and automati-
cally when the church Christ is building was faithful
to its Spirit-filled witness, not only in word and
sacrament, but by its life of fellowship—a life of love
and selflessness and concern for the needy. It was
because of this community, Luke tells us, that people
looked favorably upon the church, and it was
because of the church's reputation for joyful generosity that people flocked to the fellowship.

Other places in the Book of Acts show a surprising cause-and-effect relationship as far as evangelism is concerned. In chapter 6, the church ordains
deacons so that the daily distribution of food could
be handled more efficiently. Result: "The number of
disciples in Jerusalem increased rapidly" (6:7).

Chapter 9 tells about the church's response to the
converted persecutor, Saul. Initially afraid of him,
they eventually offered him hospitality and safety.
Result: The church "was strengthened; and encour-
aged by the Holy Spirit, it grew in numbers, living
in the fear of the Lord" (verse 31).

In chapter 16, Paul and Timothy travel through Asia Minor telling the Gentile churches about Jerusalem's decision regarding Christian unity. Because of the Jerusalem decision, Jewish and Gentile Christians could now enjoy table fellowship together. Result: "The churches were strengthened in the faith and grew daily in numbers" (verse 5).

Spontaneous Evangelism

Why were the churches growing? Not because they had evangelism programs, but because they had a reputation for fellowship and generosity, because they were hospitable, because they were concerned for unity.

This is not to say that evangelism programs are wrong. As a matter of fact, Paul indicates in his letter to the Ephesians that the evangelist is one of God's gifts to the church, to build up the body of Christ and "prepare God's people for works of service" (Ephesians 4:12). But what should give us pause is the fact that throughout the Book of Acts, evangelism is the natural result of a living church.

When the people of God are right with God and with each other, when they are growing in the faith and in the knowledge of the Lord Jesus Christ, one of the inevitable and spontaneous results is the salvation of the lost.

To put it another way, the quality of life in the Christian community was in and of itself a witness to the world concerning God's love in Christ. Such a loving community cannot help finding favor in a world rent by alienation. In the midst of an intensely lonely society, the reconciled and reconciling love of the people of God has tremendous drawing power.

By the quality of its corporate life, the church Christ is building demonstrates the relevance of God's redemptive remedy to the polarization and fragmentation of human society. The church shows the world God's way of peace.

Alienation Reversed

A secularizing influence began in the Garden of Eden when our first parents disbelieved God's word and rejected God's will, believed the lie and obeyed the deceiver. Ever since that day, our world has been torn by violence.

The alienation between humans and God issued in alienation between Cain and his brother, Abel—a division that led to murder.

It resulted in the brutality shown by Lamech as he boasted to his wives, "I have killed a man for wounding me, a young man for injuring me. If Cain is avenged seven times, then Lamech seventy-seven times" (Genesis 4:23, 24).

It led to the moral corruption in Noah's day: "The LORD saw how great man's wickedness on the earth had become, and that every inclination of the thoughts of his heart was only evil all the time" (Genesis 6:5).

It resulted in man's organizing God out of his life, collectively denying any need of God. By building the tower of Babel, man attempted to be his own god, to worship his own achievements.

According to the story in Genesis 11, "the whole world had one language and a common speech" (verse 1). God's judgment upon the tower builders was to "confuse their language so they will not understand each other" (verse 7).

At Pentecost, God reversed this judgment. "All of [the followers of Jesus] were filled with the Holy Spirit and began to speak in other tongues as the Spirit enabled them" (Acts 2:4). The crowd had no trouble understanding, "because each one heard them speaking in his own language" (verse 6). Pentecost was God's way of reversing the alienation that culminated in Babel and of reunited the fractured human family.

A Church of Peace

We live in a world that desperately longs for peace. Little wars rage within and between nations, and hanging over the whole earth is the threat of a devastating, final, totally annihilating thermonuclear war.

Despite all efforts for peace, despite all of the protests and demands and demonstrations and behind-the-scenes negotiations, war persists. It is not only war between nations or military engagements between different groups within nations. It is also war between races, between management and labor, between the haves and the have-nots, between husbands and wives, between parents and children. In spite of a universal passion for peace, wars of all shapes and sizes proliferate. In the midst of this warring world where peace seems like an illusion, Christ is building his church.

Someone will say, "The church in the world is hardly a demonstration of peace. Look at Northern Ireland, Lebanon, the former Yugoslavia. Look at the divisions among those who profess to be Christian."

Precisely! This is what humans do to the church of Jesus Christ when they try to build it themselves. This is why the church today so desperately needs, in the words of Billy Graham, to be set back two thousand years—back to the days when humans were allowing the Holy Spirit to build Christ's church.

Chapter Seven

Christ in You

Very truly, I tell you, the one who believes in me will also do the works that I do and, in fact, will do greater works than these, because I am going to the Father. . . . And I will ask the Father, and he will give you another Advocate, to be with you forever. This is the Spirit of truth, whom the world cannot receive, because it neither sees him nor knows him. You know him, because he abides with you, and he will be in you.

John 14:12, 16, 17 (NRSV)

In the upper room, at the last supper he shared with his disciples before his crucifixion, Jesus tried to prepare them for what was soon to happen. His words are recorded in the fourteenth, fifteenth, and sixteenth chapters of the Gospel of John.

Jesus knew his friends would experience severe trauma when he was apprehended, tried, convicted, and executed. He knew they did not understand the true Messianic hope as it was proclaimed by the prophets. They could not comprehend that he was the suffering servant described in Isaiah 53, that he entered history to lay down his life on the cross for the sins of humankind.

Jesus was familiar with the false Messianic hope, the product of centuries of tradition. He knew that his disciples, along with many other people of Judah and Galilee, expected the Messiah to be a political, military hero. He knew that all of them, like the outspoken Peter, repudiated the idea of the suffering servant.

Continuing Jesus' Ministry

A crucified Messiah had no place in this tradition, and apparently Jesus was never able to convince his disciples that this was his role in God's redemptive purpose. He must have discussed his forthcoming suffering and death with them many times during their three years together, but the disciples were never able to hear him. They were waiting for the moment when Jesus would lead the violent overthrow of imperial Rome and restore the kingdom to Israel.

Jesus knew that his death and burial would leave them in despair, that they were simply incapable of comprehending the bodily resurrection. So he began his last discourse with words of comfort and hope:

"Do not let your hearts be troubled. Trust in God; trust also in me. In my Father's house are many rooms; if it were not so, I would have told you. I am going there to prepare a place for you. And if I go and prepare a place for you, I will come back and take you to be with me that you also may be where I am" (John 14:1-3).

The last discourse was not designed only to comfort the disciples in their trauma and despair. It was also intended to give them hope. Jesus wanted to prepare them so they could continue the ministry he had begun. He wanted to get them ready for a greater destiny than they could possibly imagine. He wanted them to understand that his presence with them during the three years of his public ministry would be transcended by an unimaginable reality.

He had been *with* them for three years; now he was going to be *in* them. They had heard him teach, felt his love, watched his works of mercy and miracle. Now he was going to continue that ministry in and through their bodies.

Jesus and the Father

Before telling his disciples of the amazing things to come, Jesus had an interesting conversation with Thomas and Philip. Jesus had finished his words of comfort by saying, "You know the way to the place where I am going" (John 14:4)

Thomas responded with a direct contradiction: "Lord, we don't know where you are going, so how can we know the way?" (14:5).

Jesus' answer is one of the most significant statements in the New Testament. "I am the way and the truth and the life," he said. "No one comes to the Father except through me. If you really knew me, you would know my Father as well. From now on, you do know him and have seen him" (14:6, 7).

Philip was puzzled. We can imagine him thinking, *We know Jesus. We've been with him for three years. What does he mean when he says, "If you really knew me, you would know my Father as well"? And what does he mean when he tells us we have seen the Father? When have we ever seen the Father?*

Philip's response was predictable. "Lord, show us the Father," he said, "and that will be enough for us" (14:8).

We can almost feel the disappointment in Jesus' voice as he said to Philip, "Don't you know me, Philip, even after I have been among you such a long time? Anyone who has seen me has seen the Father. How can you say, 'Show us the Father'? Don't you believe that I am in the Father, and that the Father is in me?" (14:9, 10).

These questions are followed by one of the most remarkable declarations the human ear can hear and the human mind can fathom. Jesus said, "The words I say to you are not just my own. Rather, it is the Father, living in me, who is doing his work. Believe me when I say that I am in the Father and the Father is in me; or at least believe on the evidence of the miracles themselves" (14:10, 11).

Who Did They Think Jesus Was?

It would have been interesting to talk with Thomas and Philip following these brief responses of Jesus to their expressions of doubt or unbelief. If they had been asked at that point in their experience with Jesus what they thought of him, what would they have replied? Who did they think Jesus was? What was the meaning of his life? What had he come to do? What were their expectations of him, having walked with him in an intimate relationship for three years? What did they think of Jesus?

They would have seen and heard most of that which is preserved in the New Testament accounts of Jesus' life. That is to say, they would have been first-hand witnesses to most of what preachers and teachers of the New Testament draw on today for their sermons and lessons. In fact, they probably saw a great deal more.

John says at the end of his Gospel, "Jesus did many other miraculous signs in the presence of his disciples, which are not recorded in this book. But these are written that you may believe that Jesus is the Christ, the Son of God, and that by believing you may have life in his name" (20:30, 31).

Having heard all that they had heard, having seen all that they had seen of Jesus by this time, how would they have described him? Certainly they had heard him talk at length about his own purpose in entering history. They had heard much of his teaching about the Father. Mark says that Jesus "did not say anything to [the people] without using a parable. But when he was alone with his own disciples, he explained everything" (Mark 4:34).

The disciples were privy to the most intimate facts concerning Jesus and his heavenly Father. At the last supper Jesus said to them, "I no longer call you servants, because a servant does not know his master's business. Instead, I have called you friends, for everything that I learned from my Father I have made known to you" (John 15:15). What an incredible privilege!

Greater Works Than These

Now, only hours away from the beginning of Jesus' suffering, humiliation, and crucifixion, Thomas and Philip challenge him. We can be grateful for Thomas's skepticism. If he had not spoken it, we would not have Jesus' profound and reassuring response: "I am the way and the truth and the life." And we can also be thankful for Philip's ignorance, because Philip's request and Thomas's question set the scene for Jesus' astounding teaching about his plans for his disciples after his ascension.

The disciples had grown accustomed to Jesus' physical presence; now they would have to prepare for his physical absence. It was time for Jesus to talk about the church he was going to build. It was time for him to tell his friends what would lie beyond his death and resurrection. It was time to show them his plan, or, more accurately, his Father's plan.

Would the consummate witness in history of the Father in the Son end with Jesus' physical departure from the earth? Would incarnation, "truth become flesh," be a matter of only three years during Jesus' ministry? Would Christ's followers be left on their own to do their best to perpetuate the phenomenal life and teaching of Jesus? Would the full light of the Son coming into the world now diminish generation by generation, growing dimmer and dimmer, illuminating less and less of God's truth?

Jesus was about to startle his disciples—and us—with a categorical declaration that can be apprehended only by faith. Thinking about it boggles the mind. It challenges human reason. But Jesus said it, and we must deal with it. Did he know what he was saying? If he did, did he mean it just as he said it? Could it possibly be true? Do we dare take it seriously?

"Very truly, I tell you, the one who believes in me will also do the works that I do and, in fact, will do greater works than these, because I am going to the Father" (John 14:12, NRSV).

Notice that Jesus did not say *the works that I did*, but *the works that I do*. It sounds as though Jesus intends to keep on doing his works, and greater ones. Apparently incarnation of the Father in some form will go on. God will continue working in human flesh.

Our Work: Believing

"Very truly"—often translated "truly, truly" or "verily, verily"—was a common way Jesus emphasized the importance of something he was about to say. "The one who believes in me"—what a simple condition, but integral to Jesus' ministry in our midst. In the strictest sense, belief is the work.

After feeding the five thousand from one boy's lunch, Jesus commanded the people: "Do not work for food that spoils, but for food that endures to eternal life."

Confused, the people responded, "What must we do to do the works God requires?"

Jesus replied, "The work of God is this: to believe in the one he has sent" (John 6:27-29).

This is the truth that emerges. During Jesus' public ministry, the words he spoke and the works he did were the words and works of the Father, who was dwelling in him. Hence in Jesus the Father was revealed. This is why Jesus could say, "Anyone who has seen me has seen the Father." The words and works of the Father are to continue in the lives of Jesus' followers, those who believe in him. The work of the disciples is to believe. The work of the Father is to do his works and speak his words in and through all who believe.

The Spirit in the Believer

But Jesus had announced that he would be leaving the disciples. How then would the Father speak and work through them?

"I will ask the Father, and he will give you another Counselor to be with you forever—the Spirit of truth," Jesus told them. "You know him, for he lives with you and will be in you" (14:16, 17).

Something new is going to happen! He who has been *with* the disciples is now going to be *in* them. What could be plainer? The triune God—Father, Son, and Holy Spirit—will inhabit the bodies of those who believe in Jesus. He will continue the work Jesus began.

When Jesus was on the earth during his public ministry, he was limited by time and space, as are all physical beings. He could not be in more than one place at one time. Think of the potential if Jesus' physical presence could be multiplied a hundred million times so that he could work and speak in millions of different places simultaneously! What if the one who is omnipresent in the Spirit could be omnipresent in the flesh?

That is precisely the point of Pentecost. "I will not leave you as orphans; I will come to you," Jesus had promised his disciples (14:18).

When the rushing wind and tongues of fire filled the upper room, when the believers went out into the streets of Jerusalem speaking to people from every nation, they knew that Jesus' promise was being fulfilled. "God has raised this Jesus to life, and we are all witnesses of the fact," Peter said to the crowd. "Exalted to the right hand of God, he has received from the Father the promised Holy Spirit and has poured out what you now see and hear" (Acts 2:32, 33).

The Fullness of Time

Jesus Christ is the revelation of God the Father. Paul the apostle declared: "When the fullness of time had come, God sent his Son" (Galatians 4:4, NRSV).

The Epistle to the Hebrews begins as follows: "In the past God spoke to our forefathers through the prophets at many times and in various ways, but in these last days he has spoken to us by his Son" (Hebrews 1:1, 2).

Were Paul and the author of Hebrews speaking only of a brief period of three years during which God would speak through his Son? Absolutely not!

The last days, the fullness of time, began two thousand years ago with the birth of Christ. We have been living in God's redemptive plan for two millennia. The Son has continued to speak and continued to work throughout all the fullness of time, all of these last days. He will continue to work and speak until God's redemptive purpose is consummated at the second advent of Christ. He does this through the gift of Pentecost, the Holy Spirit who lives in Christ's body, the church.

The Vine and the Branches

The words and the works of Christ, begun in his own body as recorded in the Gospels, are to continue in his new body, the church. In the light of this unprecedented plan of God, it is illuminating and relevant to ponder anew a familiar portion of Jesus' last discourse to the disciples.

"I am the true vine, and my Father is the gardener. He cuts off every branch in me that bears no fruit, while every branch that does bear fruit he prunes so that it will be even more fruitful. You are already clean because of the word I have spoken to you. Remain in me, and I will remain in you. No branch can bear fruit by itself; it must remain in the vine. Neither can you bear fruit unless you remain in me.

"I am the vine; you are the branches. If a man remains in me and I in him, he will bear much fruit; apart from me you can do nothing. If anyone does not remain in me, he is like a branch that is thrown away and withers; such branches are picked up, thrown into the fire and burned. If you remain in me and my words remain in you, ask whatever you wish, and it will be given you. This is to my Father's glory, that you bear much fruit, showing yourselves to be my disciples.

"As the Father has loved me, so have I loved you. Now remain in my love. If you obey my commands, you will remain in my love, just as I have obeyed my Father's commands and remain in his love. I have told you this so that my joy may be in you and that your joy may be complete" (John 15:1-11).

Think of it! The church is *in* Christ, and Christ is *in* the church. It is absolutely necessary for believers to remain ("abide," in some versions) in Christ, and for Christ to remain in them, if they are to bear fruit. And all this began to come to pass on that incredible Pentecost morning in Jerusalem, when "all of them were filled with the Holy Spirit" (Acts 2:4).

Serving Christ in the World

From the time of my ordination in 1942 until I retired as a pastor in 1981, my entire ministry had been immersed in a "religious" environment—that is to say, an environment in which most, if not all, understood the pastor's responsibilities and, for the most part, supported him in them.

There were many things that I as a pastor could assume. I had been called by a congregation and therefore was accepted by its members as pastor. I was reimbursed by the congregation, and I was expected to do pastor-like things: preaching, teaching, counseling, calling on the sick and elderly, and so on.

When I retired in 1981 and began my work as chaplain of the United States Senate, I suddenly realized what it was like to serve Christ in a secular environment. Though I had been elected by the Senate as its chaplain, the election was routine, and most of the senators did not know me. And though they knew that the Senate had a chaplain, they expected very little from him except to open the sessions with prayer each calendar day.

None of the people on the Senate support staffs had anything to do with my position. They had not called me; as a matter of fact, most did not realize there was a chaplain in the Senate. Except for a few senators who were personal friends and a few staff members who attended the church I had pastored, I was just another face in the halls. There was little recognition of my office and less of myself as the one who filled that office.

Nothing in this new environment was remotely like the pastoral work I had enjoyed for almost thirty years. Night after night for months I would go home feeling like a mascot and wondering if I really should be in the Senate. Had it been a mistake to leave the church I had pastored for so long, and which had been such a love affair the whole time?

A Serious Relationship

In the course of this early experience in the Senate, I began to understand the position of average lay persons in the world where they spend most of their time. They are identified by the position they hold or the job that is their responsibility.

With a few exceptions, the people among whom they work are not particularly interested in their faith, their pilgrimage with Christ, their church, their beliefs. Generally speaking, any effort to speak a word for Christ, to do personal evangelism, or to witness in the conventional sense is ignored if not rebuffed. In other words, there is little if any recognition of matters of faith that followers of Christ take very seriously and treat as more important than any other issues in their lives.

Now, after thirteen years on the job, I realize that whatever I say or do as chaplain is infinitesimal in importance compared to the presence of Christ in my life. Where I have found acceptance of myself, of my faith, of those matters that are most important to me, it has not been on the basis of my office or title or my brief prayer opening the Senate. Any measure of my effectiveness during the years I've been with the United States Senate, to the extent that it can be measured, has almost nothing to do with those conventional things.

Of infinitely greater importance to whatever effectiveness I've had in this responsibility has been the fact that I take my relationship with Christ seriously. I have expected that what he will do in me and through me will be the real witness, and I have walked by faith in that confidence day by day. God has been faithful through these thirteen years; he has kept his word. And the basic discipline in my life has been to believe his word and to guard at all costs my personal relationship with him, as well as with my sisters and brothers in Christ.

The Spirit Witnesses to the Father

Today the environment in which the average follower of Christ labors, apart from his or her church work, is totally secular, materialistic, humanistic, hedonistic, narcissistic—or, to put it bluntly, pagan. How can a follower of Christ have any influence for Christ in such an anti-Christian environment? What books can one read, what methods can one learn, what seminars and workshops can one attend that will enable a lay person to witness effectively for Christ in a godless environment?

The answer, of course, is that having an influence for Christ in a pagan world is humanly impossible— "but with God all things are possible" (Matthew 19:26).

Scripture is clear: *God is his own witness in history.* If God is to be known, he must make himself known. If he is to be seen, he must manifest himself. He has done this in nature, in history, in the Old Testament through the people of God, and, consummately, in the person of Jesus Christ, the final, total self-revelation of God in history.

In Acts 1:1, Luke reminds us that what he had recorded in his Gospel was only "about all that Jesus *began* to do and to teach" (emphasis added). Obviously the doing and the teaching were to continue. Verse 8 explains how: "You will receive power when the Holy Spirit comes on you; and you will be my witnesses . . . to the ends of the earth."

Please notice that the only condition to being a witness was being filled with the Holy Spirit. In other words, just as the Holy Spirit had witnessed to the Father in the Jewish carpenter Jesus, he would continue to witness to the Father in the bodies of all Jesus' followers.

Water, Light, and Fragrance

Jesus said, " 'If a man is thirsty, let him come to me and drink. Whoever believes in me, as the Scripture has said, streams of living water will flow from within him.' By this he meant the Spirit, whom those who believed in him were later to receive" (John 7:37-39). It is a fact of spiritual truth that from the one who believes in Christ, streams of living water flow. The believer may not be aware of them, but Christ speaks the truth, and the living waters are real.

Two verses from Paul's second letter to the Corinthians illustrate this beautifully. "God, who said, 'Let light shine out of darkness,' made his light shine in our hearts to give us the light of the knowledge of the glory of God in the face of Christ" (4:6). Like the living water flowing from us, the light of Christ shines through us.

"Thanks be to God," Paul writes, "who . . . through us spreads everywhere the fragrance of the knowledge of him" (2:14).

If we look at these verses we realize that God is the subject. God is the one who is causing the light to shine, the one who is diffusing the believer's environment with the fragrance of the knowledge of Christ. God is the one who is acting. He is the doer. We are only "jars of clay," "earthen vessels" in the familiar words of the King James Version (4:7).

This means that the streams of living water, the light of the knowledge of the glory of God, and the fragrance of the knowledge of Christ are manifested unconditionally. They depend only upon God's action. Our responsibility is simply to believe what God's Word says.

Believe Christ, believe the promises, depend completely upon that which God will do in us, to us, for us, and through us. It is not what we do for God in the world that matters; it is his witness to himself. It is what we allow God to do in us and through us that influences our behavior, our attitudes, and our words.

To put it another way, our witness to Christ is the witness of his presence in us. It is his loving, saying, and doing in us. We are not even conscious of most of what he is doing in us. And none of it, incidentally, is measurable.

Chapter Eight

Salt and Light, Seed and Yeast

You are the light of the world. A city built on a hill cannot be hid.
No one after lighting a lamp puts it under the bushel basket, but
on the lampstand, and it gives light to all in the house. In the
same way, let your light shine before others, so that they may see
your good works and give glory to your Father in heaven.
                                        Matthew 5:14-16 (NRSV)

Where does the church of Jesus Christ touch the world with its maximum influence?

Is it at the denominational level, with the ecclesiastic institutions? Is it the pronouncements and resolutions that come from its annual, biannual, triennial, and quadrennial gatherings? Does its greatest influence come from its executives and administrators, its presidents and bishops?

Is its major influence due to the local church—the church on the corner with its impressive buildings, its so-called campus, its senior pastor and corps of clergy specialists, its programs for every age and human condition?

Does it best influence the world through its various programs for outreach by local churches and parachurch groups, through mass movements, great evangelistic crusades filling huge stadiums, or television or radio broadcasting that reaches millions?

Is its influence chiefly due to the pastors of the small churches that comprise ninety-five percent of the churches in America, or the thousands of faithful missionaries serving Jesus Christ in unknown, unsung, difficult areas, or the indigenous ministries of third-world churches?

The Influence of the Scattered

Important as are all of the people and organizations we have just mentioned, their influence is infinitesimal compared to the influence of the aggregate of individual believers committed to Christ under the control of the Holy Spirit, working wherever they are, penetrating all the social and institutional units of our world between Sundays.

The true measure of the church's influence is what is happening when the buildings are empty, the programs idle, and the people scattered throughout their communities, metropolitan areas, and the world.

In other words, the real influence of the church is not what is happening when the church is visible in its buildings. The real influence occurs when the church is invisible, when it is in dispersion.

Israel did not have its greatest impact on history when it was consolidated and visible as a nation, even under the reign of King Solomon, Israel's golden age. Israel had its greatest impact on history when it was in *diaspora*, when it was scattered and, as a nation, invisible.

In dispersion, Israel brought to the whole world its Scriptures, its God of revelation, its moral law, and its messianic hope. In exile, Israel had prepared the whole world for the coming of the Messiah, for the birth of Jesus Christ. The wise men from the East are examples of Gentiles who, thanks to the influence of the Jews in dispersion, had searched the Scriptures and were awaiting the newborn King.

On the day of Pentecost, "there were staying in Jerusalem God-fearing Jews from every nation under heaven: . . . Parthians, Medes and Elamites; residents of Mesopotamia, Judea and Cappadocia, Pontus and Asia, Phrygia and Pamphylia, Egypt and the parts of Libya near Cyrene; visitors from Rome (both Jews and converts to Judaism); Cretans and Arabs" (Acts 2:5, 9-11). Upon hearing the testimony of the 120 disciples freshly filled with the Spirit, three thousand of these devout Jews were baptized. We can assume that after the feast these Jews returned to their own lands, which means the church of Jesus Christ was begun in each of these places.

Benevolent Subversion

Four images given by our Lord himself illustrate why his people in all ages have been most effective when they are dispersed into the world. Salt, light, seed, and yeast do their real work when they are invisible. Salt in the shaker, light covered, seed in storage, yeast in the pantry are useless unless they are taken out and allowed to penetrate their environments, becoming invisible.

The influence of the church in the world is not to be understood so much as an army marching with banners flying, but rather as a kind of secret service penetrating and benevolently subverting the institutions of the world, which belong to our Lord's enemy.

Some time ago it was my privilege to speak to a meeting of Christian Educators in America during their convention in Washington, D.C. In preparation I read that there were 330,000 Christian teachers in public schools in the United States. Wanting to be sure of the accuracy of that statistic, I asked one of the officers of the association. He told me that their estimate was nearer 500,000.

Think of it! Half a million Christian teachers penetrating, permeating the public schools of our land. Their influence for Christ is enormous—and yet it is invisible, unmeasurable. And we have become such victims of the visible, the measurable, the quantifiable, that we talk and act as though the battle for public school education is already lost.

Is Jesus Christ, who indwells those half a million teachers in our public school system, doing nothing while they are in the schools? Is he speaking and working through them only when we can see and quantify and measure the influence they are having?

And what about the millions of Spirit-led, Christ-filled believers penetrating most of the other institutions of the world—business, industry, the professions, entertainment, agriculture, science, construction, homemaking, service clubs, the universities, government, the military—you name it.

Christ has his people everywhere. They are penetrating, permeating, pervading most if not all the units of the social order like salt, light, seed, and yeast. And they are having a quiet, effective influence for Jesus Christ continually, not sporadically, not only when they do something visibly religious.

The Work of the Church

Perhaps it would be helpful at this point to make a distinction between *church work* and *the work of the church*.

Church work is what is done for the religious establishment—the building, the organization, the programs. In the most active churches, it requires fewer than ten percent of the members to keep such activities going.

The work of the church, by contrast, is the work in which the church is involved when it is scattered between Sundays in the world. The work of the church requires every member of the church, every day.

One of the most remarkable laymen it has been my privilege to know was a young dentist, Jimmy Sheets, a member of the First Presbyterian Church of Hollywood. He was a godly man, unusually faithful in his church attendance and in church activities. He was a deacon and was very active in a group of young marrieds called "The Home Builders," from which much of the church leadership came. Jimmy never missed a service Sunday morning, Sunday evening, or Wednesday evening if he could possibly help it. He was the kind of church member one depended on whenever there was a need to be met.

Once when he was working on my teeth, he said he wanted my counsel about something. He had been asked to be president of the Board of

Education of his community, Inglewood, a southwest suburb of Los Angeles. The work required and the social activities connected to it, he said, would make it impossible for him to be as active in the First Presbyterian Church of Hollywood as he had been in the past.

How Many Members Does It Take?

As Jimmy began to describe the activities from which he would have to withdraw, I felt anger rising in my heart. I resented the Board of Education of Inglewood. How unfair for this secular organization to rob the First Presbyterian Church of Hollywood of one of its finest members! But the work being done on my teeth made it impossible for me to respond.

As I seethed inwardly in silence, God began to speak to me. It was as if he asked me a question: "How many members are there in the First Presbyterian Church of Hollywood?"

I answered, "Eight thousand."

God asked, "How many of those members does it take to run the establishment of the First Presbyterian Church of Hollywood?"

I made a rough estimate and said, "Eight hundred."

"What about the other seven thousand, two hundred members of the church?" God asked. And then, "Wouldn't it be wonderful if every Board of Education in every city in the United States had as its president a godly person like Jimmy Sheets? Would that not have a remarkable spiritual and moral effect upon education in all of these cities?"

When I was able to respond to Jimmy's question, I told him I felt it would be wonderful if he would accept the responsibility of being president of Inglewood's Board of Education.

The Church in the World

I returned to my office after the dental appointment, sat down and began to figure out how many people it would take to run the First Presbyterian Church of Hollywood if each person could have only one job. For example, a church officer could not teach Sunday school. A choir member could not be a deacon. Only one church job would be allowed per member. On this basis, it turned out that to run all the activities and programs and organizations of the church would require something less than seven hundred people. How were the thousands of others to be involved?

It was then that I realized my mistake. As pastor, I was behaving as thought the church were in competition with all the other organizations in the city. I realized how much I had resented this competition. I had assumed that if there was a church activity when the Rotarians met, a good believer would be in church, not at Rotary, and I felt this way about every other organization in the community. If a church member was more active in the community than in the church, he or she was doing the wrong thing. That organization was stealing one of our members.

Thank God for my experience in the dental chair! For it was then that I realized that the real work of the church is in the world, when the church sanctuary and classrooms are empty and the people of God are scattered. The church is doing its most significant work when its members are busy with their jobs, their schools, their service clubs and school boards and community projects.

To put it another way, the church of Jesus Christ is doing its work when it is invisible.

Salt and Light

In his Sermon on the Mount, Jesus declared categorically to his disciples: "You are the salt of the earth. . . . You are the light of the world" (Matthew 5:13, 14). He did not say "You *ought to be* salt and light" or "*Try to be* salt and light." He simply said, "You *are* salt, and you *are* light."

Can food resist the salt that has been sprinkled on it? Does darkness have any power against light? If you opened a door between two rooms, one dark and the other light, would the darkness rush in and suffocate the light, or would the light rush in and dispel the darkness?

The answers are obvious. Food has no power whatsoever against salt, and darkness is helpless before light. The smallest flicker of light is invincible against the darkness, and the smallest Christian witness will have its effect on the world.

Jesus admonished his disciples, "Let your light shine before others, so that they may see your good works and give glory to your Father in heaven" (verse 16, NRSV). Notice the interesting relationship between light and good works. The text implies that some good works glorify the worker rather than God because light is absent, while other good works glorify God rather than the worker because light is present. This suggests that when our light is shining, people are not particularly aware of us, any more than they are aware of light when it is illuminating its object.

It is only when the light is not shining properly that people are aware of it. When it flickers or goes out suddenly, we are conscious of the light, but when it shines, we notice what it is illuminating. And so it is with us as disciples. When our light is shining, people see God's work and not ours.

The Good Seed

The thirteenth chapter of Matthew records a parable Jesus told about the kingdom of God: A man sowed good seed in his field and, while he slept, an enemy sowed weed seed. When the seed began to grow, the servants noticed the weeds in the midst of the wheat. They informed the farmer of this and asked if they should pull up the weeds. " 'No,' he answered, 'because while you are pulling the weeds, you may root up the wheat with them. Let both grow together until the harvest' " (verses 29, 30).

He explained the parable to the disciples: "The one who sows the good seed is the Son of Man; the field is the world, and the good seed are the children of the kingdom; the weeds are the children of the evil one, and the enemy who sowed them is the devil; the harvest is the end of the age, and the reapers are angels" (verses 37-39, NRSV). The followers of Christ, then, are as good seed planted in the soil of the world by Christ.

Does the soil have any power whatsoever over the seed to prevent it from germinating and producing?

As we answer this question, we must remember the other parable about seed Jesus told in Matthew 13. In it, the seed is the word of God, and the soil is the human heart. There are four kinds of soil: hard, shallow, thorny, and fertile. Although the soil itself does not have power over the seed to prevent its growth, it may contain elements that can interfere. But the qualifying factor is that Jesus is the sower.

Like a wise farmer, Jesus knows his soil. Whether he is planting the word of God in the human heart, or his followers in the world, it is safe to assume that he plants good seed where he knows it will produce. And Jesus has the right to expect a harvest.

Now the question again: Does the soil have any power over the seed to prevent it from germinating and producing? Our Lord said in another context, "Unless a kernel of wheat falls to the ground and dies, it remains only a single seed. But if it dies, it produces many seeds" (John 12:24). The problem is not with the soil, but with the seed itself. If it will not die, it cannot produce.

To answer the question: Just as the soil cannot prevent the seed from doing its work, neither can the world around disciples where Christ has planted them prevent them from doing their work.

Don't Rush the Harvest

The Enemy sows weed seed where the Lord has sowed good seed, perhaps with the design of suffocating the seed and making it unprofitable. Those of us who are good seed, planted where we are by the Lord Jesus, will be surrounded by weeds planted there by the Enemy. Like Jesus himself, we cannot and should not expect always to gain friendly acceptance from those with whom we labor day in, day out. We should not be surprised when our associates express displeasure at our way of life, our habits, our occasional verbalizing of the gospel of Jesus Christ and what it means to us personally. Weeds there will be.

It may seem sometimes that they suffocate us and make it impossible for the life in us to produce the harvest Christ intended when he planted us where each of us is. The text indicates, however, that the weeds do not have this power over the good seed.

Jesus said that the harvest is the end of the age. With that in mind, it is certainly premature to try to ascertain, before the end of the age, the real measure of the harvest. At a time when the church has been so tragically infected by the secular way of measuring effectiveness, looking for results that are measurable, visible, tangible, and quantifiable, it is important to keep Jesus' words in mind.

Jesus also said that the reapers are the angels. They are the ones who separate the wheat from the weeds. As a pastor, I have observed over the years that the weed pullers in the church are a problem. They think they are cleaning up the field, but in the process they damage the wheat. It is not harvest time yet, and we are not angels. It is not our job to count and sort the plants growing in the field.

Quietly Changing History

In another parable in Matthew 13, Jesus described the kingdom of God as "yeast that a woman took and mixed into a large amount of flour until it worked all through the dough" (verse 33). Does the flour have any power over the yeast? Can it keep it from doing its work? The answer, once again, is obvious.

My favorite devotional writer, Oswald Chambers, has a line in *My Utmost for His Highest* that I like. It can apply to salt in the food, light in the room, seed in the soil, and yeast in the dough. Chambers says, "Never allow the thought, I am of no use where I am; you certainly are of no use where you are not."[1]

The church Christ is building is an invisible, invincible force in society because he is building it. Human institutions and effort may fail, but it is inconceivable that Jesus would fail to do what he declared he would do. The world has no power over his church, just as food has no power over salt, darkness no power over light, soil no power over good seed, and flour no power over yeast.

As salt, light, good seed, and yeast, the church that Jesus Christ is building permeates the world and changes history. This is something to be believed, not because we see the evidence of it (although evidence is there), but because Jesus said so. Even though circumstances may indicate the contrary, we choose to believe the word of Jesus against whatever the world may show us.

We are salt, light, good seed, and yeast, and we are quietly doing God's work.

Note

1. Oswald Chambers, *My Utmost for His Highest* (Westwood, N.J.: Barbour and Company, Ltd., 1963).

Chapter Nine
You Will Be My Witnesses

That which was from the beginning, which we have heard, which we have seen with our eyes, which we have looked at and our hands have touched—this we proclaim concerning the Word of life.

1 John 1:1

Y ou will receive power when the Holy Spirit comes on you; and you will be my witnesses in Jerusalem and in all Judea and Samaria, and to the ends of the earth" (Acts 1:8). These were Jesus' words to his disciples just before he ascended into heaven.

The word *witness* is fundamental in understanding the influence of the church in the world. The Holy Spirit was given at Pentecost so that Jesus' followers could witness to him. Because of the strategic importance of this word, it is important that we consider it as objectively as possible, free from any traditional biases or prejudices or understandings we may bring to it.

There are at least four aspects to witness: proclamation, performance, penetration, and presence. Each is a form of witness, and we will look at the nature of each one.

Witness Is Proclamation

The gospel of Jesus Christ has to be *proclaimed*, told, verbalized. The apostle Paul, in his Epistle to the Romans, asks, "How can they believe in the one of whom they have not heard? And how can they hear without someone preaching to them?" (10:14, NRSV).

On the day of Pentecost, each of the 120 disciples witnessed in a different language to those who were gathered in Jerusalem to celebrate the feast. On that day Peter preached a sermon that led to the baptism of three thousand people.

The deacon Stephen preached a powerful sermon that resulted in his death, but that also may have influenced the later conversion of Paul.

Another deacon, Philip, explained in words the gospel of Jesus Christ to the Ethiopian eunuch.

Paul himself communicated with words: he wrote, he preached, and he taught.

And certainly following the persecution in Jerusalem, as the believers were scattered to different cities and countries, wherever they went they told the story of Jesus Christ.

God's words have been transmitted to writing, and we have them in a book that can be read, heard, studied, and discussed.

Witness Is Performance

Yes, witness involves words, but witness is infinitely more than words. Words were not adequate even for God. John declares in the first chapter of his Gospel, "The Word became flesh and lived for a while among us. We have seen his glory" (verse 14, NRSV).

Witness is something to see as well as to hear. Witness is performance. None of us would argue with the cliché, "What you do speaks so loudly that I cannot hear what you say." God has given us ears to hear what is said, and he has given us eyes to see what is meant by what is said. The visual context of words has a great deal to do with what they communicate.

Paul, in his classic statement on salvation by faith, indicates this: "It is by grace you have been saved, through faith—and this not from yourselves, it is the gift of God—not by works, so that no one can boast. For we are God's workmanship, created in Christ Jesus to do good works, which God prepared in advance for us to do" (Ephesians 2:8-10). Clearly good works witness to our salvation, to our being new creatures in Christ Jesus.

James certainly had this in mind when he wrote, "Faith by itself, if it is not accompanied by action, is dead" (James 2:17). Incidentally, the issue here with James is not works but faith. The faith James proclaims is manifest by works. If works are absent, obviously something is wrong with the faith. James is not advocating salvation by works; he is advocating salvation by the faith that makes itself known through works. His words are similar to those of Jesus in John 7: "Whoever believes in me, as the

Scripture has said, streams of living water will flow from within him" (verse 38).

To James, works are the evidence of faith. How else do we prove our faith but by our works? We have been saved through faith and created in Christ to do good works. Faith in God generates good works. Jesus told us to let our light shine so that people might see our good works and glorify the heavenly Father. Certainly performance is witness, and words without performance are not necessarily witness.

The words we speak as Christ's witness gain their significance to those who hear them by our performance, by our good works, by our love. Our behavior at home, at the daily task, in the neighborhood, among friends and strangers—this is a powerful witness to our faith in Jesus Christ, to our new life in him.

Witness Is Penetration

In the last chapter we looked at four images Jesus used to explain the kingdom of heaven: salt, light, seed, and yeast. All of these images involve penetration. Salt in the salt shaker is useless. Light covered is useless. Seed in the storehouse is useless. Yeast in the cupboard is useless.

Salt penetrates as it is sprinkled on the food; light uncovered penetrates the darkness; seed scattered penetrates the soil; and yeast penetrates the flour. Penetration is necessary, or the work will not get done.

Jesus does his work in the world as his people penetrate into all parts of society. Dispersed into the world, they will have an influence that only eternity can evaluate.

If we had tried to measure the results of Jesus' three years of public ministry right after his resurrection, we would consider them a failure. At best, there were five hundred disciples; only 120 gathered in the upper room. Even the twelve were not totally faithful. One betrayed him; one denied him; and all but one abandoned him when he hung on the cross. Jesus had ministered to the multitudes in love. He had healed them, fed them, cared for them, and taught them. But he died nearly alone on the cross as though no one cared.

The effectiveness of the life, works, teachings, death, and resurrection of Jesus Christ can be measured only in terms of all the things that have happened in the centuries and millennia that have followed. His followers have penetrated the world to such an extent that today, nearly two thousand years later, one quarter of all human beings call themselves Christian.

Witness Is Presence

Imagine what it must have been like to be with Jesus. It would have been exciting to hear his remarkable words, to see his extraordinary deeds. But how wonderful just to be with him, to feel his presence!

All of us have experienced the power of presence. Each of us can think of people who make a difference when they enter or leave a room. Their presence charges the atmosphere, even if they do not say a word.

There are times in life when presence alone is relevant. When a friend is going through a deep personal tragedy, when a spouse has lost a loved one, when a parent has lost a child, when a friend has lost a good friend, usually words do not help. Often they hurt. But personal presence can be filled with meaning, comfort, and healing. Presence communicates care, love, concern, and availability. There is no substitute for presence, and presence is witness.

The apostle John sums it up: "That which was from the beginning, which we have heard, which we have seen with our eyes, which we have looked at and our hands have touched—this we proclaim concerning the Word of life. The life appeared; we have seen it and testify to it, and we proclaim to you . . . what we have seen and heard" (1 John 1:1-3).

Witness is not just something to hear. It is something to see, to handle. It is tangible and material. The apostles had very little theology at the time of Jesus' death on the cross. They knew very little about him, and they did not understand the little they knew. They were crushed and confused by his death, and they could not comprehend that he would rise again. But they knew him!

For three years they had been with this incredible man. They were often mystified by what he said and did, but they knew that he was real, he was loving, he could not be ignored. He—and not simply facts about him—was their message. Jesus witnessed to God by the power of his presence.

Not Materialistic Enough

We often hear that the church is too materialistic, and in one sense that is true. Nevertheless, it is not materialistic enough when it thinks of witness only in terms of words, theology, doctrine, or preaching.

Too often we communicate to the world a formula or system to be believed rather than a person to be received, to be trusted, to become a friend. In our zeal to defend the deity of Jesus Christ, we lose his humanity, forgetting that when God wanted to reveal himself supremely to the human race, he did so in a human body.

The first heretics in the Christian church did not deny the deity of Jesus Christ; they denied his humanity. Gnostics taught that somehow matter was evil and spirit was good, and the two could not be mixed. Therefore Jesus, who was divine and spiritual, could not at the same time be human and physical. His body was not a real body; it only appeared human.

This heresy denies the goodness of God's creation. Genesis 1 records that "God saw all that he had made, and it was very good" (verse 31). When God wanted to manifest himself, to reveal himself supremely to those he loved in the world, he impregnated a virgin's womb and a child was born.

The child grew up to be the man Jesus, a carpenter's son from the rough hill town of Nazareth. This man was the supreme witness in history of almighty God. God's way to witness to himself was not to transcend history but to indwell history. Through Jesus Christ, God became a material presence among us.

Too Materialistic

We Christians are too materialistic when we are friends with this world. Wanting the world to be friends with us, we attempt to do God's work the world's way. We measure the value of God's work by the world's criteria.

Wealth, health, and security have become very important to many of us. It is easy to overlook statements such as these by Jesus and his disciples:

"If the world hates you, keep in mind that it hated me first" (John 15:18).

"In this world you will have trouble. But take heart! I have overcome the world" (John 16:33).

"Do not love the world or anything in the world. If anyone loves the world, the love of the Father is not in him" (1 John 2:15).

"Don't you know that friendship with the world is hatred toward God? Anyone who chooses to be a friend of the world becomes an enemy of God" (James 4:4).

We have adopted the world's love for statistics and use them as virtually the sole measure of the effectiveness of a pastor, a form of witness, an evangelistic program, or a church.

A common concern I have had to deal with during most of my fifty years in ministry has been the discouragement many feel because they haven't won as many to Christ as someone else, or because they have seen very few measurable results from their desire to be a witness for Christ where they are daily. They hear the testimony of someone who has led a number of people to Jesus Christ, and they begin to question their own effectiveness.

I recall one dear friend, who was as deeply spiritual as anyone I've ever known. She shared with us how, during her time in Bible school, she was required to report each Monday morning in class how many she had "won" to Christ the night before.

It was not uncommon for her to get out of bed Sunday night and go back into the street to "win" somebody so that she could give a good report to her class the next day.

Numbers can be very intimidating, very discouraging to a faithful servant of Christ when they are interpreted as the measure of effectiveness in witness.

Wait for the Harvest

In the parable of the wheat and the tares, Jesus explicitly stated that the good seed and the weeds were to be allowed to grow together until the harvest, which he identified as the end of the age.

In another parable he spoke of a man who, before leaving town, gave his servants money to invest. "'Put this money to work,' he said, 'until I come back'" (Luke 19:13). Notice that the accounting was to wait until his return.

The apostle Paul said that "the creation waits with eager longing for the revealing of the children of God" (Romans 8:19, NRSV), for the time when the created world "will be liberated from its bondage to decay" and our bodies will be redeemed (verses 21, 23).

It is a joy when we are told that people have come to Christ. But any estimate of the effectiveness of our witness at this time is premature. One day we will stand before the Lord Jesus Christ to give an account of the deeds done in the flesh. Only then will each of us know how Jesus has worked through us in the lives of those in whose midst we have lived and labored.

We can be grateful and rejoice when we know of one who has been blessed by our lives in Christ. But we must understand that we walk by faith in this matter, as well as in other matters, waiting for the final accounting at our Lord's return.

Chapter Ten

The People of God

The gifts he gave were that some would be apostles, some prophets, some evangelists, some pastors and teachers, to equip the saints for the work of ministry, for building up the body of Christ.

Ephesians 4:11, 12 (NRSV)

The church of Jesus Christ does not make its maximum impact on the world through its so-called professionals—preachers, pastors, evangelists, missionaries, directors of Christian education. It makes its greatest impact through its lay people.

It is through the people of God, in whom Christ dwells through his Spirit, that he speaks his word and does his work. The people of God influence the world for Christ wherever he has sent them, wherever he has planted them. Through his people, Christ is infiltrating all the units of society throughout the earth.

Wait for the Spirit

Following our Lord's bodily resurrection, he spent forty days in precious fellowship with his friends before his ascension. During this time he taught them many things about the kingdom. But most importantly, he exhorted them to wait for the baptism of the Spirit.

Why should they wait? They had all the data. They had been with Jesus for three years, hearing what he taught, seeing what he did. They had gone through the trauma of the crucifixion and burial, the euphoria of the resurrection. They had all the facts. Why weren't they ready now to go out and tell the world about Jesus? Why wait for the Holy Spirit?

Jesus made it clear that witness was impossible without the Spirit. Though they had all the information, they were to wait for the power, the life, the presence. Witness is more than information. Witness is incarnation.

In the New Testament, witness is really the Holy Spirit witnessing in and through the lives of believers. To be more explicit, it is the manifestation of the life of God—Father, Son, and Holy Spirit—in the lives of believers wherever they are, whatever they do.

This witness is not limited to religious or spiritual matters. It is in all of life. The Holy Spirit witnesses in the body of every single believer, every moment of every day with every breath he or she breathes, every word he or she speaks, everything he or she does. This assumes, of course, that the believer walks in the Spirit, that nothing mars his or her relationship with the indwelling Christ, that Christ is in control of his or her life, and that he or she is submitting to God's will.

The work of ministry is the responsibility of every believer.

Every One a Minister

Paul states this explicitly in the fourth chapter of his letter to the Ephesians. Every one of us has a sacred vocation, or calling, he says. Each of us has been prepared for this sacred vocation by a measure of grace. When Christ ascended to heaven, he gave gifts to the church.

"The gifts he gave were that some would be apostles, some prophets, some evangelists, some pastors and teachers." In other words, he gave leaders to the church. But these leaders were not to be the church's primary ministers. To the contrary, they had a specific assignment: "to equip the saints"— that is, the lay people—"for the work of ministry, for building up the body of Christ" (Ephesians 4:11, 12, NRSV). Clearly in the apostle Paul's understanding, the work of ministry is the responsibility of the people of God.

What, then, is the work of ministry? In the first place, the word *minister* means "servant." To minister is to serve. It doesn't simply mean to do something religious; that false view of ministry comes from the false dichotomy between the secular and the sacred.

In Matthew 25, our Lord separated the people into sheep and goats on the basis of how they served. He said to the sheep, "I was hungry and you gave me something to eat, I was thirsty and you gave me something to drink, I was a stranger and you invited me in, I needed clothes and you clothed me, I was sick and you looked after me, I was in prison and you came to visit me" (verses 35, 36).

The people were amazed at his words; they had no idea they were serving Christ. But Jesus explained, "Whatever you did for one of the least of these brothers of mine, you did for me" (verse 40). Helping others is ministry to Christ. It is ministry just as much as telling somebody about the gospel or preaching a sermon or teaching a Sunday school class or singing in the choir or serving on the official church board.

Not that these church functions are unimportant. Thank God for them and for those who are dedicated to doing them. But were are never to equate witness or ministry simply with religious things. Ministry is what we do to and for Christ in others every moment of every hour of every day, with every breath we breathe and every step we take.

Jesus on the Job

In his enthronement sermon, the Bishop of Winchester, England, said, "For most people in the diocese of Winchester, Hampshire and even Dorset, it's only one end of the [train] line. For the commuter, the company directors, stock brokers, members of the Lords or the Commons, civil servants, lawyers; for the seamen, the dock workers at the container ports, and the halyer; for the farmers and market garners, the other line matters enormously. A great part of life is lived there. And according to the promise of the risen Christ, that is where we can discover for ourselves that he is indeed alive and powerful."

The bishop told of a friend of his, a priest who works in London, who was invited to lead a discussion every Wednesday evening during the six weeks of Lent. It was a wealthy parish, and most of the men who joined the discussion worked in London's financial district. The priest chose as his theme, "Christ at Both Ends of the Line."

Jesus, said the priest, is really alive and at large in the world. What kinds of questions is he bound to be asking about the objectives of a large corporation and its methods of achieving them, about its responsible use of resources, about its use of the time of the people it employs? The priest then showed from the Bible what Jesus must want from his followers in the financial district.

Not surprisingly, the executives got angry. They did not think the church had any business meddling in their daily affairs. The priest sadly concluded, "The church as a whole still prefers to meet Jesus Christ behind the closed doors of its own weakened Jerusalem and does not want to find him alive in the Galilee of the job, of politics, and of international affairs."

The Christ of Galilee

Later in his sermon the bishop said, "It is going to be painfully hard to turn around and run counter to all the assumptions and habits of the working world. It is going to cost more than ordinary courage can bear. And it is precisely at this point that we shall either prove or disprove that Jesus is alive. For we claim not only that he makes us see things in a new light, but he sets us free to do things in a new way.

"It is easy enough to recite that in the religious environment of our Jerusalem, but it is in the

Galilee of politics, commerce and international affairs that we actually put his resurrection to the test. So this is not a shallow gospel of social reform. I am talking about repentance, faith, forgiveness, salvation in the critically realistic terms the world understands. It is for the honor of our Saviour that we must go and find him in Galilee. . . .

"Many of us who have known and loved our Lord for many years in the Jerusalem of our private religious life are in need of a further and deeper conversion to the Christ of Galilee, the secular world where people are expected to keep religion out of it. . . .

"Lord Jesus Christ, alive and at large in the world, help me to follow and find you there today in the places where I work, meet people, spend money and make plans. Take me as a disciple of your kingdom, to see through your eyes and hear the questions that you are asking, to welcome all men with your trust and truth, and to change the things that contradict God's love. By the power of the cross and the freedom of your Spirit. Amen."

Small Is Beautiful

Despite all our protestations against materialism, secularism, and humanism in the last two decades, the fact is that, perhaps more than at any other time in history, the church has taken the way of materialism, secularism, and humanism. In our religious lives we have learned to quantify everything. Statistics have become the last word in measuring effectiveness, and the bottom line is the ultimate evidence of success. All our criteria for a successful church or pastor are materialistic—the size of the building, the size of the congregation, the size of the budget, the number and diversity of our programs.

Fifty percent of the churches in America have an attendance (not membership) of seventy-five or fewer people each week. Thirty percent have an attendance of from seventy-five to two hundred. Fifteen percent have a weekly attendance of from two hundred to three hundred fifty. That leaves only five percent with an attendance of over three hundred fifty. Of these, a mere handful have an attendance of over two thousand.

We ought to rejoice in the large churches and not criticize them. The problem is that the evangelical community has been unconsciously infected with the idea that the large church is the model for all to follow. It is assumed that a young pastor, upon leaving seminary, will either go from a small church to a larger and then a still larger church, or will move from being a staff member to being a senior pastor. Such "upward mobility" seems to be the test of the pastor's effectiveness as a servant of Jesus Christ.

No one ever says this, of course. It is never verbalized. But it is implicit in much of our thinking and planning. We can see this kind of thinking in the church growth movement. Growth and effectiveness are assumed to be quantitative, rarely qualitative. Meanwhile tens of thousands of faithful servants of Christ go from seminary to ordination to the grave, pastoring a small congregation. By our contemporary criteria of churchmanship, these pastors must be unsuccessful and ineffective.

The Body in the World

This is a destructive way of thinking. Even more destructive is the fact that many lay members, like the average pastor, assume they are serving Christ only when they are involved in the big program. Busy with organizations or committees that are doing church work, they rarely if ever realize that their influence for Christ where they are, day in and day out, is probably more important than anything they do in and for the religious institution, or in the various programs designed to help them do ministry.

Too often lay members don't think of the influence they are having through character, attitude, and response to those in need. They discount the impact of a loving and caring and forgiving spirit, the desire to help others, and a willingness to listen. They don't realize they are being the body of Christ when they are a friend in a world that is friendless, when they love in a world starved for love.

They don't see their ministry as related to how they, as employers, treat their employees or customers; how fair, honest, and just they are in their business dealings; what they do with their profits. Or, if they are employees, they don't see their ministry as a matter of being faithful at the task for which they are employed and for which they receive wages.

Buicks and Bibles

Some years ago I was asked to speak at a seminar on lay ministry during a National Association of Evangelicals convention. Following my remarks, I opened the floor for questions and comments. The first to stand was a man who said, "I am a Buick dealer, and I run my Buick dealership as a ministry for Christ."

All of us were curious, so I said, "Tell us how!"

He responded, "I give Bibles away." That was the end of his comment.

I said, "Sir, I would not offend you for the world, but I believe that when you stand before the Lord Jesus Christ to give an account of the deeds done in the flesh, he will not question you concerning the number of Bibles you gave away. He will ask you how you conducted your Buick dealership, how you ran your service department, how you treated your employees, how honest you were with your customers, and what you did with your profits."

Needed: Righteousness Lessons

There is only one essential in equipping the saints for the work of ministry: training in righteousness. It is almost impossible to understand how the evangelical community seems to miss this.

In his Sermon on the Mount Jesus commanded, "Strive first for the kingdom of God and his righteousness" (Matthew 6:33, NRSV).

Paul's statement to Timothy, which is prescriptive for evangelicals and is taken as seriously as any passage of Scripture, makes this point: "All Scripture is inspired by God and is useful for teaching, for reproof, for correction, and for training in righteousness, so that everyone who belongs to God may be proficient, equipped for every good work" (2 Timothy 3:16, 17, NRSV).

Paul described his own ministry this way: "We proclaim him, admonishing and teaching everyone with all wisdom, so that we may present everyone perfect in Christ" (Colossians 1:28).

Twice in the beatitudes Jesus mentions a blessedness

associated with righteousness: "Blessed are those who hunger and thirst for righteousness, for they will be filled," and "Blessed are those who are persecuted because of righteousness, for theirs is the kingdom of heaven" (Matthew 5:6, 10).

In that context Jesus added, "You are the salt of the earth" and "You are the light of the world" (verses 13, 14). Is it not fair to assume that being salt and light have to do with one's desire for righteousness?

Certainly this is implied when Jesus says, "If the salt has lost its taste, how can its saltiness be restored? It is no longer good for anything, but is thrown out and trampled under foot" (verse 13, NRSV). We can safely deduce that when the salt has lost its saltiness, no program and no activity can compensate for it. Saltless salt is simply good for nothing.

Method and Mystery

In our love affair with the institution, we have reduced everything to methodology. A person who is trained in ministry or who has been discipled is one who is trained in some method. Witness has become an acquired skill.

We have been inundated with how-to books in the past two decades: how to study the Bible, how to pray, how to lead someone to Christ, how to disciple another. You name it, there is a book written on how to do it.

The absurdity of the how-to syndrome dawned on me when I noticed in a bookstore a number of titles telling people how to be born again. Pondering these volumes, I remembered that Nicodemus once asked Jesus: "How can anyone be born after having grown old? Can one enter a second time into the mother's womb and be born?"

Jesus answered, "The wind blows where it chooses, and you hear the sound of it, but you do not know where it comes from or where it goes. So it is with everyone who is born of the Spirit" (John 3:4, 8, NRSV). That was Jesus' answer to the question, How can one be born again? One sentence. And in that sentence, he suggested that the new birth is a mystery.

The how-to syndrome has mixed effects. Some think that once they have learned to apply a method, they will get the desired results. This belief is especially strong in the area of personal evangelism. And yet during his public ministry, Jesus was rejected by more than accepted him. If the number responding affirmatively to a ministry is the criterion of success, then Jesus Christ himself was a failure by contemporary standards.

The how-to syndrome produces another undesirable effect. Too many lay members will excuse themselves from ministry because they think they don't know how to do it. They have not been able to attend a training seminar or discipling course, so they excuse themselves from any responsibility for influencing the world for Jesus Christ.

As a consequence, multitudes of laity suffer a constant low-grade guilt. Hearing the testimony of those who used a method and reaped dramatic results, they consider themselves failures. Impressed with the quantitative results of others, they attach no value to their influence for Christ on a day-by-day, hour-by-hour, moment-by-moment basis, wherever they are and whatever they are doing. They assume that the only criterion for effective ministry is using a method in order to gain the desired results.

The Ministry of the Laity

What about righteousness? Where is the righteous housewife, mother, father, or neighbor? The righteous school teacher, business executive, sales associate, or dentist? The righteous government official, professional athlete, truck driver, or waitress? Where are the righteous?

A 1970 editorial in *Christian Century* declared: "There is no greater operational failure in American Christianity than the failure to make the ministry of the laity a visible reality. Not all our talk about the church's mission, nor the new evangelism, nor the new games in Christian education, nor the crash programs on the crisis in the nation, nor our ecumenical spectaculars can bring much health to the body of Christ unless the meaning of the laity as ministry is incarnated in the style and structure of our common life. . . .

"Clergy are tempted to focus the laity's attention on the needs of the parish church. The result is that only one form of ministry is affirmed. And those laity who feel called to minister primarily within the world of work are marginalized and made to feel guilty."

Bill Diehl, in *Christianity and Real Life*, makes this operational failure personal. He writes: "I am now a sales manager for a major steel company. In the almost thirty years of my professional career, my church has never once suggested that there be any type of accounting of my on-the-job ministry to others. My church has never once offered to improve those skills which would make me a better minister, nor has it ever asked if I ever needed any kind of support in what I was doing. There has never been an inquiry into the types of ethical decisions I must face, or whether I seek to communicate the faith to my co-workers. I have never been in a congregation where there was any type of public affirmation of a ministry in my career. In short, I must conclude that my church really doesn't have the least interest in whether or how I minister in my daily work."

Turn from Your Wicked Ways

Most of the laity have been called to spend most of their time in productive labor in a career to which God has led them. They are doing the work of ministry every minute they are doing the task to which they have been called. The question is, Are they doing it righteously? Is it not conceivable that right here is the crux of our dilemma in contemporary evangelicalism—righteousness?

Since two or three years before the bicentennial, as evangelicals began calling our nation back to its biblical and spiritual roots, the text of 2 Chronicles 7:14 has been quoted thousands of times: "If my people, who are called by my name, will humble themselves and pray and seek my face and turn from their wicked ways, then will I hear from heaven and will forgive their sin and will heal their land."

Multitudes of revival-hungry people, longing for a genuine, heaven-sent spiritual awakening, say "Amen" when they hear that text. And yet somehow the awakening does not come.

There has been an extraordinary revival of evangelicalism, including the remarkable charismatic movement that crosses all denominational lines and touches millions of people. Yet social evils—the dysfunctional family, divorce, permissive sex, crime, drug dependency, wife and child abuse, rape—grow exponentially.

Over the last twenty years many people, including a president of the United States and a convicted Watergate conspirator, have witnessed to being born again, but during the same time period, social conditions have worsened. Is it conceivable that we have not been turning from our wicked ways?

Indifference to Justice

When we think of wicked ways, we think instantly of personal morality—illicit sex, marital unfaithfulness, abortion. Most of us who are yearning for revival are not guilty of that kind of sin, generally speaking. So there is really nothing for us to turn away from. The evil must lie somewhere else.

But is it possible that the wicked ways from which we must turn are more subtle than we usually think? Could they include the worldly ways of thinking—the materialism, the secularism, the humanism—that have so badly affected evangelicals in the last couple of decades?

Is it conceivable that our love affair with bigness, the spectacular, the dramatic; our adulation of the celebrity and the superstar; our readiness to equate these things with effective influence for Jesus Christ in the world—is it possible that these are the wicked ways from which we must turn?

In the original biblical languages, righteousness and justice come from the same root. Is it possible that our indifference to justice—our neglect of the poor, our lack of concern for the oppressed, the imprisoned, the hungry, the malnourished—is the wicked way from which we must turn before God sends awakening and heals our land?

We do seek his face. We do pray. We do humble ourselves. But we continue so often in a selfish, hedonistic, narcissistic way of life, chiefly interested in being comfortable in this life, in acquiring as much as possible, in being successful and important and popular. Is it possible that these are the wicked ways from which God is asking us to turn?

Standing in the Gap

What would happen if the people of God longed for righteousness? What if we really hungered and thirsted for righteousness? What if more than anything else in life we desired the kingdom of God and the justice that comes with it? What if we sought to be pure of heart and meek? What if we were willing to suffer for righteousness' sake? What if justice was more important to us than anything else in life?

One cannot help thinking of the story of Abraham when God told him his plan for Sodom (see Genesis 18:20-33). Abraham, concerned especially for his nephew, Lot, and his family, prayed that God would spare the wicked city.

Abraham asked, "Will you sweep away the righteous with the wicked? What if there are fifty righteous people in the city? Will you really sweep it away and not spare the place for the sake of the fifty righteous people in it?"

The Lord agreed to spare the city for fifty righteous people.

Supposing, said Abraham, there are only forty-five? Or forty? Or thirty? Or twenty?

The Lord agreed to spare the city for that many righteous people.

Then Abraham said, "May the Lord not be angry, but let me speak just once more. What if only ten can be found there?"

The Lord said, "For the sake of ten, I will not destroy it."

Where are the righteous? One of the saddest verses in the Bible is in Ezekiel 22:30 where God says: "I looked for a man among them who would build up the wall and stand before me in the gap on behalf of the land so I would not have to destroy it, but I found none."

What tragic words. God could not find ten righteous in Sodom, and he could not find one righteous in Jerusalem.

What if each of us, wherever God has placed us, however powerful and popular and prominent or humble and out-of-the-way our position, would say to the Lord, "When you look where I am to find one who will stand in the gap against the destruction of the land, Lord, let me be that one. If you will save the city for the sake of ten righteous, Lord, let me be one of the ten."

The Church in the World

Strive first for the kingdom of God and his righteousness, and all these things will be given to you as well.

Matthew 6:33 (NRSV)

It is a matter of eternal significance when a lay believer enters into his or her daily task. The lay believer may be
president of the corporation
or custodian of the building housing the corporate offices,
a United States senator
or a food service person,
a parent staying at home with the children
or a parent going to work to provide for them,
a single person obeying God's call
or a retired person who cares about other people.

Whoever the lay believer is, whatever he or she does, one thing is certain: when the lay believer enters into his or her daily task, the work of the church is being done.

The only valid measure of the programs inside the church buildings is the righteousness of the believer at his or her common task during the week when the church buildings are empty and the programs inoperative.

The lay believer is fulfilling the divine call, his or her sacred vocation, not by taking time out of the daily routine to do something religious, but by faithfully doing his or her secular work, performing the task as a servant of Jesus Christ to the glory of God.

The real impact of the church of Jesus Christ in the world rides on the quality of the lay believer's life in the daily routine.

Jesus commanded, "Go and make disciples" (Matthew 28:19). The rhythm of the church is gathering and going, worshiping and working, meeting together in order to be equipped to disperse, to disappear as the church in the various organizations and institutions of the community. Like salt on food and seed in soil, the church penetrates the world into which Christ sends it.

Each believer is somewhere at all times. And wherever the believer is, he or she embodies Christ, who is never idle. In and through the people of God, by the power of the Holy Spirit, Jesus Christ today is doing the same work that he did two thousand years ago in the carpenter's body.

And that is the witness of the church in the world!